# HOW TO EAT AN ELEPHANT

## THE BUSINESS GROWTH MANUAL - VOLUME 1

## BALA K N

Made with ♥ on the Notion Press Platform
www.notionpress.com

*To my Family*

# Contents

# Acknowledgements

Let me start by expressing my gratitude to the Almighty for being the inspiration, the soul and the wisdom behind everything that is found here, thank you God!

Next, but equally in my gratitude, I would like to thank my wife, who has stood by me all these years, for the quiet love, patience and for always inspiring me with a sense of a grander purpose and for always standing by me with support and reassurance that have given me the strength and conviction to take up this endeavour and see it to completion.

To my son and my daughter for their love, patient support, and their constant words of encouragement for me in my journey as a writer.

To my friends who have come into my life over the years, who have let me learn from them, and who have been there when I needed them most.

To my clients, mentees, and professional colleagues for their inspiring stories, of triumphs and failure in business, and of survival against the worst odds, who have let me study and delve into their businesses, all of which have helped evolve my perspective and understanding of how successful businesses grow, evolve and thrive. It is an honour to have been a part of every single one of your journeys.

# Preface

In the course of their entrepreneurial journey, every entrepreneur is faced with diverse challenges that unfold from time to time posing questions that demand answer and which ultimately form the basis of their major and minor decisions.

Sound decision making becomes most critical when the decision involves substantial financial investment and fund deployment. Wrong or misplaced choices and decisions can mean loss of capital, higher expenses, wastage of resources, besides loss of time, all of which can result in impactful losses.

When the basis of the decision itself is wrong, the decision results in avoidable 'adverse outcomes', in other words business losses.

This affects small businesses who have limited 'capital sources' substantially, especially small SME businesses who are in the life line and cannot afford to make mistakes.

On the other hand, decisions that were based on the right understanding, rather than hearsay truths, caused the decisions to produce favourable results and envisaged outcomes for the business.

It is observed that businesses which were more organised with better structure, processes and management made better decisions that considered the pros and cons, while being holistic, and this resulted in better outcomes and higher performance 'predictability'. This made the business more valuable and well in control, in the hands of the management.

Less 'organised' and 'unstructured' businesses conceived 'ideas', created products and solutions, but were not able to produce 'success' or predictable 'financial outcomes'.

Businesses that planned and seriously applied themselves to envisioning and quantifying goals, strategizing, and performing could actually produce success.

Businesses where the team worked cohesively in a 'common single direction' had a higher chance of success.

It is true that people from all walks of life, wade into entrepreneurship setting up and thus creating business enterprises. The way they set up and manage their businesses and take the most and least consequential decisions is often based on their own ideas and understanding, the majority of which are gathered in the course of their professional life or their area of occupation while many younger first time entrepreneurs having landed in entrepreneurship directly from campuses look to adapt or apply their course material, often hurriedly and without due consideration, to their business ventures.

It is a fact that as an entrepreneur your mind is filled with ideas, dogmas, 'understandings' and opinions. Your Business decisions based solely on the above may produce mixed and unpredictable outcomes which are, more often than not, 'adverse' in nature.

For many entrepreneurs, these misplaced ideas and 'understandings' did not help them to bring out the grandest version of their business and themselves, and also did not help them to express and realise their true potential through achievement of the business goal and meeting the larger business purpose. Thus, through this perspective, entrepreneurs rely on myths rather than observation, logic, understanding and objectivity.

In other words, their 'understandings' about what serves their business and what may not serve their business is more limited than they could ever know. Many of the 'understandings' were themselves entirely based on 'what was in the past' rather than 'what is there today', and often based on 'someone's opinion based on what existed in the past' rather than 'truth based on logic' and changed 'present reality'.

In this way, entrepreneurship carried the legacy of earlier generations of businesses who passed on practices that limit the potential of the business enterprise. While they may realise, eventually, that these practices are not serving them, they continue to dogmatically hold on to such practices.

As a result, entrepreneurs remain stuck at one point, unable to take timely business decisions. This causes businesses to miss a lot of opportunities, waste a lot of time and expend scarce financial resources even as the entrepreneur dogmatically holds on to past ideas and 'understandings', old truths and old myths, none of which are any longer relevant in the new changing business context.

Entrepreneurs often cause crises to occur in their business by their acts of omission or commission, find themselves in adversities of their own making and eventually shy away from shouldering responsibility for business failure that is often attributable to their own actions.

**What does this book aim to convey?**

This book is the first of a three-book volume and seeks to address and unravel many myths, misconceptions, impressions, and beliefs that entrepreneurs may have in their minds, which haven't led them to where they wanted to be.

This book strives to provide answers to the questions that occur to every entrepreneur.

Questions that entrepreneurs normally have like:

What went wrong with my business?

Why am I not able to make it?

Particularly hard to find answers for day-to-day business problems, both mundane and complex.

Provide practical solutions to address the challenges and pain-points suffered by businesses for which business owners may not be able to gather practical and contextual answers that perfectly fit their quest for solution.

*While exploring the experiences, observations, rules and practices that serves the wellbeing of businesses, this book provides answers to questions which enable entrepreneurs to produce the highest success for their businesses by taking advantage of favourable market trends and by preventing failure in the most adverse of business and market circumstances.*

*So, this book is original in its perspective.*

This book relies on my practical knowledge, observations and analyses obtained through an extensive career dealing with diverse businesses, research, studies and learnings gained regarding wrong practices that made businesses fail, and the best practices that successful businesses leveraged to produce success. Hence, on some or many of the topics, it may be at variance with the conventional understanding and commonly published beliefs and may be considered as a different point of view.

This book aims to express complex principles in simple terms, lay down vital principles, and time-tested practices that can enrich the governance of a business organisation.

This book collates the information into a well-arranged manual that makes it easy for entrepreneurs to absorb, analyse, engage with, and implement *to produce* business transformation and the *highest success outcome for their Business.* This book examines every facet of the business and provides a step-by-step approach to deal with failure producing factors which entrepreneurs can adopt in order to avert business failure and lead their businesses to success.

Everything that is being said here needs to be read and internalised in that context with a keen and open mind, new-preparedness and new-perspective. This book seeks to invoke preparedness in the mind of every entrepreneur to be open to new understanding, new truths, new wisdom, new practices, and even new paradigms which could serve the business and lead the business in the envisaged direction.

This book is here to inspire and 'call to action' every entrepreneur in business and to tell the aspiring entrepreneur that the 'world of business' awaits your entry, and that you do not need to be afraid, afraid of falling, you no longer need to work to avoid failure, instead, cause the circumstances to occur which make success possible. In doing so, you are urged to always follow your heart, identify your true passion, shape your purpose and then set out to build your great entrepreneurial dream through your inner strength and empathy and move in the direction of your goal.

## Who should read the book?

This book is for entrepreneurs managing small and medium-sized enterprises, and start-ups looking to become bigger and move into a growth trajectory. This book is for a new entrepreneur looking to set up their maiden business venture, professionals and ex-employees considering a foray into entrepreneurship, for entrepreneurs running existing businesses that are making losses and are financially stressed, businesses which are not performing due to high manpower attrition, businesses with high debt burden looking to reduce debts, businesses looking to raise capital, businesses seeking help to quantify business goals, create a business plan and formulate strategies for their business, and lastly students looking to entrepreneurship as a career choice and so on.

This book keeps the challenges of all the above categories of entrepreneurs in mind whiling discussing principles, concepts, views, ideas, observations that are aimed at guiding entrepreneurs and their businesses to actualise their true potential and move on the definitive path of value creation and financial abundance.

This book is dedicated to each and every entrepreneur on the face of the earth.

This book is dedicated to every student who is a future entrepreneur, in order to empower them to be able to create strong, powerful and successful business enterprises.

Once again, I am dedicating this book to every entrepreneur with great aspiration, belief and desire, that they will find all or at least some of the material contained in the book worthy of adopting in their businesses...

# CHAPTER ONE

# THE JOURNEY

A child was once asked a question by his teacher, "Son, can you eat an elephant"? The little boy thought about it for a little while and said, "oh, I certainly cannot, for the elephant is big and I am so small".

On hearing the child's reply, the teacher said "My dear child, if you truly desire it, you can certainly eat an elephant, but you will have do so, piece by piece". She continued "yes, it may take you a while, depending on your appetite, but you can". And then the teacher added, 'If you have the intent, there is nothing that you cannot achieve".

This book is not about elephants!

This book is about 'perception.'

**Power Of Perception**

Your perception determines your thoughts. Your thoughts create your vision for your business which leads to the goals which emerge from it and all this ultimately results in your experience of success in your business.

Thus, it is clear that to experience success in your entrepreneurial life, you must have the right perception. Even after having all the competence, the technical skills, the innovation ability, the entrepreneurial spirit and the most important thing being 'passion' for the business, if you cannot believe in yourself you cannot succeed. If you do not have the will or the tenacity to turn your aspirations into a solid goal, you are about to experience the biggest loss in your life.

If you do not dare to see the goal in the eye, that your ambition and passion wishes to show you, it is possible that you will cast your vision too low. And that is what you will create,' mediocrity' and 'disillusionment'.

Commitment to excellence, not mediocrity.

Yet as an entrepreneur, you must remember the truth that mediocrity does not define 'who you are'.

You are here to create an extraordinary story of entrepreneurship, saga of business success, enviable wealth creation, social empowerment and so on.

In your entrepreneurship you cannot be limited by anything for too long, you do have the access to the knowledge ,the wisdom, the tools to craft your entrepreneurial journey and the way to lead your venture to success path.

You only need to sharpen your observation, your listening and propensity for learning by adopting knowledge, wisdom and practices that serve your business and implement them and thus lead your business in its journey to the destination called 'success'.

**New thoughts and new ideas**

If you observe that a certain past understanding is not valid any more, with the passage of time and the changed circumstances, there is no harm in altering your understanding. If a certain principle that you held close to you in the past no longer serve you, then don't hesitate to replace it with new understandings, observations and experience. This is the sure way to success.

In reality most entrepreneurs fear to reflect or introspect on their past actions and reject the thought or realization that they have been making bad decisions all borne from absurd and illogical assumptions which caused the loss or failure to occur.in this way entrepreneur and members of senior management fail to own their mistakes. As a result of the denial many entrepreneurs experience failures one after the other in serial order. All the while they deny that they had anything to do with such adversity, every time failing to notice that it was they who were causing the failure.

If it is not possible to attribute the failure to any other person, then they would in all likelihood attribute the failure to act of god or fate.

Not owing the responsibility for the mistake or omission thus deny these entrepreneurs the opportunity to change the circumstances that caused the mistake or omission to repeat and occur again in their particular business. Thus, they are not able to leverage failure to draw the lessons that would help them to succeed, the next time.

From this place of inner self denial, they fail to accept 'What is really so' and hence they cannot even know 'What really works'.

You only need to have the intent to succeed. The intent has a way , it will express itself as passion, perseverance, determination, clarity of thought, incessant actions and so on. Intent and deep rooted passion can produce the opposite of ego centricity and can even stop you from your denial mode.

**The power of Passion**

Passion reassures you that compared to what you can achieve what you have achieved is not anything. Passion produces a sense of humility to see things not with fear, but with strength, to see mistakes as an opportunity and not as a reflection of more failure.

Thus Passion and culture that percolate from the founders and top management level to the team, have the ability to influence the minds of the team and galvanize 'team spirit' while producing favorable transformation for the business, necessarily in the right direction.

The good news is that the entire world was produced in this way , out of raw undiluted passion to begin with. Now it your turn. Are you going to deny and prove your theories, or drive your entrepreneurial life with passion, tenacity and determination, all the way to the goal? And this was the question that unfolded for every entrepreneur.

For every visionary entrepreneur , at first the goal looked unsurmountable, too huge, too unachievable , too formidable like an 'elephant'.

For you this limiting perception created the illusion that your skills, competence , experience and everything that you can mobilize through the power of observation, new learning , and timely actions and so on is no match when measured with the loftiness of the vision and the goals. Hence you are afraid to even speak about your true inner aspiration which forms the material of who you are.

In other words your Goal is that which defines who you are.

Goals become achievable when they are divided in to smaller parts , dismembered in to tinier less complex, visible , distinguishable and quantifiable parts which you may otherwise term as 'sub goals' for the purpose of clarity.

Setting sub goals produce more visibility, granularity on the particular aspect or the sub element of the business and thereby help in goal achievement.

Successful businesses have established the principles of strategic Business management the benefits of engaging strategy as a long term approach for accomplishing the business goals. Strategy approach along with action planning that ensure that the strategy is converted in to executable actionable items with time frames and budgeted financial impact.

Thus painstakingly strategies were formulated for each and every facet of the business such as sales, operations, delivery, innovation, human resources and so on, clearly defining the business objectives and the strategies being translated as action plans with stipulation of the team member responsible for the action along with the time frame for completion of the action item, and the financial resources budget required to accomplish the activity.

**Importance of processes and systems**

The larger more organized, successful businesses showed the way to how a business that had a solid framework of processes and systems could ensure and maintain steady performance in all spheres of activity and the contrary that businesses that lacked processes and systems indeed were unstable and often losing its direction and thus depleting the most scarce financial resources that it possessed by accumulation over the passage of time.

This dispelled the argument of those entrepreneurs who trivialized planning as unrequired activity and wastage of time advocating their philosophy that success was attained even without engaging a structured approach. Yet it is true that businesses which produced success across a time period merely by the confluence and occurrence of diverse favorable factors struggled in later years to repeat the same and failed.

In this way, entrepreneurs understood the real way to 'Plan direct and regulate' the pace of their growth to attain the highest and the most optimum performance that their goals helped to quantify. Through planning, businesses could bring great predictability period on period basis and year on year basis in their key performance parameters while also ensuring consistency not withstanding market trends that were less than uniform nor consistent.

This was the 'mantra' that all small businesses could internalize and adopt diligently in their business to break the barriers of perception and the limitations of process that restricted their growth and fulfil what they came here to achieve, the aspiration to become 'big 'and 'ever bigger' business.

They learnt the way to eat the elephant!

As they grew their 'growth appetite' grew. But they always knew the way to go. They knew how to devour even 'when the elephant got bigger'.

After all they were in the destination that many called 'success' and that was all that really mattered. They were truly the 'big business' and not losing their 'merit', they remained so, almost perpetually. For they knew how 'not to fall', how to 'stay there' ,'hold on', 'not regress'.

## Lessons from successful businesses

These lessons from their experience is there for all to assimilate, observe reflect with their own experience. That too, without slipping into a sense of self denial. Denial and incrimination was not necessary, all that was called for was to 'notice the truth' and 'live the truth' by doing what works for your business.

This is not to say that the businesses that failed did not contribute to the wisdom and the knowledge repository?

Just as the businesses which succeeded contributed many jewels of knowledge and wisdom, as well as desirable practices and unavoidable rules for managing businesses, the businesses which failed also contributed archives of data containing adverse experiences produced out of omissions and commissions, bad decisions and erroneous actions that that do not serve business and are best avoided.

Much of the insightful research findings concerning failed ventures indicated that there were two types of failures one which was caused by factors which were avoidable and the other which was caused by factors that were unavoidable or in other words not caused as direct consequence of any action of the business or the entrepreneur instead by some natural calamity or untoward accident etc.

## Definition of an entrepreneur

Yet to cognitively understand the world of business, the rules of entrepreneurship the lessons about 'success producing practices' and comprehending the essence of 'failure causing decisions' the entrepreneur has to be in the right state of mental preparedness and the person had to be truly an 'entrepreneur'.That leaves us with the salient question namely 'is every business person an entrepreneur? or in other words the question that begged an answer really was 'who could be really called an Entrepreneur' ? 'what are the qualities required for this so called 'human being' to be named ' Entrepreneur' ?

There were more questions like, is the 'founder entrepreneur' like the 'captain of the ship' ? does the 'entrepreneur captain' possess the qualities needed for an entrepreneur?

In reality, it is self-evident that 'what the 'Entrepreneur - Captain' is thinking saying or doing is important for the business entity .This decides upfront which way the business is likely to head, to the destination that is called 'Success' or any other destination which only offers adversity and loss in varying degrees. Yet this is not to mean that no one other than the Entrepreneur Captain is important, and the truth prevails that the 'entire team' who are assisting the captain is equally important for the success outcome.

Businesses are essentially 'people centric' and in that sense it is about how people come together and form cohesive teams by building strong relationship and thereby working towards the destination which is called 'goals'.


**Background and Qualities of an Entrepreneur**

The next question after analyzing the entrepreneur qualities that ideally an entrepreneur should possess we come to one more salient question ?

How did that person come to possess qualities that he displays while in their entrepreneurial stint ? did they acquire these qualities during the earlier occupation or stint in a trading business field prior to entering the field of entrepreneurship?

In other words many of them were earlier in employment, as technicians or executives while many others were practicing professionals while yet many others may have moved directly from educational campuses being students after their graduation to become entrepreneurs .In all the cases it is true that their previous background influenced their decisions while in their entrepreneurial life. Intrinsically 'how they think' 'what they think' depended on their 'location', where they came from which means whether them moved from being an employee or a professional or straight from the educational campus.

First generation entrepreneurs understand business, their relationship to business in a different way as compared to their peer entrepreneurs who may have a background of their family being from a business background. Their past exposure greatly influence their behavior and outlook in their handling the entrepreneurial role.

Entrepreneurs who have been technicians in their earlier stint in employment are more likely to be hands-on with technical matters and may have the approach of 'do it all by myself approach', may create a culture that does not promote delegation as a natural process. This culture will inhibit team work and may really become a limitation for the business in later years as the business begins to see its solutions becoming more popular with the possibility for more and more potential customers and more business.

## Business Growth stages and thresholds

As businesses evolve and grow in to becoming bigger and bigger versions of themselves particularly in terms of its physical dimensions whether it is assets infrastructure or team size and so on and scale of their financial accomplishments they however pass through growth thresholds or growth stages.

Each stage or threshold is clearly identifiable much as in the case of humans like 'life stages' of 'childhood' 'adolescence' 'youth' and so on. Just as in human parenting the parents need to prepare for every new stage of growth and face the new challenges that unfold as the child moves from Childhood to adolescence and then to youth organization, in the identical way the business enterprises also pass through growth stages or thresholds of growth. Upon the business entering the next growth threshold, the business faces new experiences and challenges, new opportunities and new threats many of which could be unfamiliar to them. Many businesses being unaware of this phenomenon, do not prepare themselves or their business for meeting the internal changes and business transformation demanded by the new growth threshold or the new growth stage.

## New challenges, New questions

Yet some businesses even view the new and different experience as a potential threat rather than the natural outcome of a simple law exercising itself or a natural growth phenomenon acting out and thus fail to assume the right mindset namely that 'it is okay for businesses to face new questions , new challenges' and that there is no need to look at them as 'negative' or 'adverse' when they look at the potential business opportunity that new stage of growth has to offer.

Thus the questions that entrepreneurs seek answers for constantly changes as they grow and evolve and in the process of their finding themselves in different and mostly new situations.

In other words, the questions that the entrepreneur seeks answer for when they are in the early start up stage is different from the questions they may have in the growth stage. This means that the current stage in which the business is placed and the entrepreneurs background may influence their question.

## Testing and validating strengths

Yet as the business evolves through the aforementioned phase systematically all the aspects of the organization is put to test whether it is the business potential of the business in general , the entrepreneur's skill and attributes like passion ,perseverance and determination, the quality of the product or the delivery, the technical capability or the technology, team strength and so on.

How they fair in dealing with the test on their aspect holistically will decide the outcome?

## Importance of team management

When businesses become physically larger it becomes necessary for the entrepreneur to find ways to keep their 'flock' or their team cohesively ' together'.In hindsight , the same three people 'startup business' started one year back now became a 'thirty person' 'Business organization'. This transformation now called for new approaches from the entrepreneur to deal with the 'organisation' consisting of many persons with diverse skill sets.

## Holistic approach to Business

From the organization standpoint the word 'Business transformation' and the word 'holistic' has a distinct connection. When you talk about a 'business organization' you have to imagine a 'tree' with 'roots' and the 'stem' and the 'leaves' the 'flowers' and the 'fruits' all having separate 'identity' and 'description' and 'role' and 'function' and of course the splendor but all 'connected together' 'nourished together' making the 'great tree what it is, namely 'the tree'.

Here we see what the word ' Holistic' really mean, and this is true of the organization cannot understand the tree and its existence if you do not understand the inter dependencies, synergies, complimentary nature of its parts and how they serve each other and serve the larger purpose, which the trees stands for.

The nature of cohesiveness between the parts, even keeping their diversity, but being inclusive even as the parts are exclusive, represent the great dichotomy.

This is true of organizations as well.

## Key elements of the Business

Understanding a business and evaluating its performance will necessarily require that there be need for knowledge of the key elements of the business like the business entity, the assets of the business, products and solutions offered by the business and so on.

You cannot control the whole when you cannot identify the parts. The parts of the business which are the elements of the business. Unless you understand the elements and their role in the working and successful outcome for the business .

## Internal Alignment of departments

All the departments of the organization exist together in harmony and functionally aligning to each other and providing the complimentary and synergistic nature and thus collectively producing the business outcome that the business stands for. And if holistic view is overlooked, the business suffers as a result.

Sales decisions and strategies concerning the sales department which overlook operations and delivery department of the business is less likely to accomplish the end purpose of achieving business goals. Similarly, decisions taken in operations department which overlooks the imperatives about team availability or business decisions concerning new product development without alignment to financial R&D budgets and working capital do not produce the desired outcomes, instead the initiative only lead to cash burning.

It needs to emphasized that when the idea of the 'core essence' of the being which is 'holistic' is overlooked, business decisions however 'dynamic' and 'lofty' it may be in its 'purpose', how much 'financial capital' may have been deployed in trying to fulfil it, at the end of the day it fails because the truth is that everything affects every aspect and everything is connected inseparably, hence overlooking or ignoring 'one part' will produce the impact of overlooking 'everything'.

## Business Equilibrium

Business success and organizational performance become the clear outcome when all the decisions taken and actions performed in the business spring from this understanding in other words the 'need for balance and equilibrium', the 'importance of alignment' and 'symmetry' while taking business decisions, the inseparable connect between 'business management and financial management', the balanced understanding of the word 'financial discipline and financial prudence' and the implications of overlooking even 'obvious self-evident' 'business truths' that have the potential to produce 'disproportionate adversity' and 'loss' for the business. To trivialize these principles while managing the organization or taking business decisions that are mostly not well founded and arbitrary produce least informed choices which cause businesses to experience failure.

## Choice of legal entity

Discussing about a holistic approach to business growth and the need for total alignment of all facets of the business to the strategic business goal it becomes relevant to mention about the importance of aligning the stage of growth of the business and its scale to the business entity structure which is called the 'Legal entity structure' .Organizations are inherently businesses which are clothed inside a legal entity which may be incorporated entity or a non-incorporated firm structure and so on. As the organization grows it becomes necessary to review whether the stage of growth align with the structure of the legal entity. As businesses grow organizations need to review the need for transformation from a non-incorporated firm structure to an incorporated structure that will align and serve the imperatives and opportunities now provided by the business growth .

## Dual Role of the Entrepreneur

The relevance of the entrepreneur knowing how to manage a business is paramount to the success of the business enterprise. Intrinsically the founder entrepreneur can be considered to dealing with two distinct roles which may in certain situations or certain time context may producing completely distinct and different perspectives and thereby different decisions.

The entrepreneur founder is an investor of his money and savings and the guarantor of all the money that the business would have raised from different sources. Besides the above the founder as the investor of company is also indemnifier of all the obligations due to the creditors and suppliers of the business in the event of default. The founder entrepreneur also has a duty to the invested capital in terms of being able to generate a return on investment (ROI) on the amount invested in the business. Thus have a fiduciary role with respect to their business.

On the other hand, the founder entrepreneur also has a different role. As the CEO(chief executive officer or (COO) chief Operating Officer of the Business or the General Manager of the business he is also a business functionary handling sales or operations or delivery or HR. While handling the aforementioned role he may have perspectives and opinions which will be anchored around the specific department concerned which may drive his decisions while playing this Role. Some of these decisions may not be validated when it is viewed from the angle as the 'investor of money'.

Entrepreneurs have to continuously deal with this dichotomy and always take a balanced and well considered , well informed view considering all aspects while taking decisions.

Intrinsically, thus the founder entrepreneur can be considered to be dealing with two distinct roles which may in certain situations or certain time context may produce completely distinct and different perspectives and thereby different decisions.

Founder entrepreneur mind becomes the mind of the business enterprise. If they are not balanced and incapable of handling their emotions and ensure the right work life balance in handling their own life, they are more likely to produce adverse influence on the team members. This could become a limiting factor for the business as a whole if the importance of mental wellness is not given the right priority.

**Lacuna in Financial planning**

When entrepreneurs are able to source capital or debt funds for their business, they are never in doubt that they know how to use the money for their Business. At that point it does not occur to them that the capital could be lost if they do not have a solid business plan and financial budgeting or a quantified goal or multi-pronged strategies and may not be aware about the ramification of not having clarity on actions items, and imperatives for having a robust business process framework within the organization.

And yet in a tearing hurry, they empty the entire fund it to their business which is not even ready for the financial infusion. As the natural outcome they mostly lose the entire capital.

## Lacuna in Operations and Delivery

Similarly, when entrepreneurs succeed in getting orders for their product or solution they are never in doubt about their capacity to deliver the products to the customer in time. Yet due to lacuna in the operations model or quality issues and so on and combined with poor financial discipline and financial management lead to haphazard and arbitrary decision making on the business front. As an outcome , these businesses fail to deliver the order to the customers in time and even fail to collect the order proceeds from the customers.

When these adverse occurrences recur more number of times in the particular business, the organization faces failure.

It does not occur to them that perhaps there is something that they did not know or missed about managing money or managing their operations or their business as a whole. And these entrepreneurs who are in denial mode attribute this business failure to adverse market circumstances or any other imaginary reason or action of an unrelated third person, always any other person other than themselves , and thus miss the whole point .They deny that they had anything to do with the business failure that their actions caused.

## Factors that limit a small business from becoming a 'Big business'

There are certain key aspects which limit the growth of small businesses in their journey to becoming larger businesses. These aspects can be traced to some controllable factors namely lack of business and Financial Planning, Lack of financial discipline. Lack of common direction, measurable achievable goals and a strategy approach of executing the business plan, lack of processes and a proper business structure and so on. Similarly, business ownership structure and choice of legal entity combined with lack of collateral securities may become some of limiting factors for facilitating equity and debt fund mobilization for the small business. Lack of skill among entrepreneurs and inability to organize a team adversely impact the business. Limited access to capital when combined with Economic downturns become the impediment to sustain and grow the business.

**Small to big - eating the elephant**

Entrepreneurs with limited means and great ideas are often unsure of themselves, and many of them even do not believe in themselves. They are limited by the resources that they have in relation with their vision for their business, they are also apprehensive about the disproportionately high amount of capital that will be required to translate their 'business idea' in to a 'product or solution' and to take the product to the 'market' and generate 'sales revenues' .

The task and the mission before the entrepreneur looked 'too daunting' and 'too formidable', 'too insurmountable', 'almost unachievable' particularly when the entrepreneur looked at the future through the 'shadow of limitations'.This 'perception' of limitation thus produced their experience of being a 'Small business' with a great idea and a 'path breaking solution' that did not dare to 'push the boundaries' and 'look beyond' and thereby strive to get to the place where the business belonged.

In this way for many 'visionary entrepreneurs' their 'passion' knew no bounds and with exceptional tenacity and conviction, in a step-by-step manner they achieved success going all the way to building most valuable unicorns and business enterprises that stood as the invaluable global brand leaders in their respective fields. This is also considering the fact that they started with 'meagre capital' at the inception of their business. We are referring to the exceptional stories of entrepreneurs like Jeff Bezos, Bill gates, Mark Zuckerberg, Jack Ma, Steve Jobs and Larry page who are founders of startups such as Amazon, Microsoft, Facebook, Ali Baba, Apple and Google and so on.

## Judgement about business success and business Failure

Mostly failure is received with fear and denial and with a prior judgement that it is wrong to fail or failure is bad or you will be judged for your failure and so on. So individuals move in to a denial mode and instead of taking responsibility and accountability for the failure place the burden on one another person who may not have directly contributed to the failure, not even taken the original decision which resulted later in failure. Here it needs to be reemphasized that in this way such entrepreneurs thus lose control to change the circumstances that caused the failure in the first place and face failure again and again in their entrepreneurial life.

For any intensively active and focused business organization, failures occurring in its way is a natural occurrence. They know and realize that the adverse outcome does not make the business fall. And when the entrepreneur come from the right place of understanding, failure itself becomes a business opportunity.

Those who understand the factors which could have been controlled and own up their mistakes are more likely to never repeat the mistakes. similarly understanding the factors that cannot be controlled makes the business always remain in a state of readiness to deal with unexpected situations.

The difference between failed business and successful business is not that successful businesses never failed. The difference is that successful business deployed failure in a different way to galvanize and materialize the thing called 'success' perpetually learning from past mistakes.

Identical businesses in identical industry verticals being peer businesses with more or less same size emerged out of adversity with different results and outcome, one failed to the extent of extinction, another emerged out of the adversity, smiling, not giving up and now clearly knowing how to succeed. Many businesses failed to understand that failure in one department is the failure of the entire business, and no matter the smallness and the importance attributed to a particular department in the business, every department in the final analysis every department has the potential to cause the business to fail, once again the importance of understanding the interdepartmental alignment become paramount.

Let us turn our attention from businesses which failed to businesses which succeeded?

## Repeating Businesses Success

An organization's capacity to repeat success year after year will depend on the one most important aspect, that is, when it is able to realistically observe and understand why the business succeeded in the first place, in other words, the answer to the question namely 'what contributed to their success'? If they realistically understood why they succeeded in the first place, they will be able to follow the steps the practices and the understanding which produced the success in the first place. Yet, many entrepreneurs may not observe and deeply analyses why they succeeded .

Businesses succeed because of many reasons, one among them being the positive confluence of favorable business circumstances. Whether these occurrences or circumstances will repeat is not known.

They may conclude that their decisions and strength are the true reason for the success, they may undermine the value of best management practices or the role of strategic approach to drive business success and may fortify and support their theory that planning, strategy process are not required for business success.

In this way many entrepreneurs may choose to deny that favorable market factors are driving the current business traction and may even dismiss the expert analysis that the positive trend is a temporary phenomenon that may not last beyond a brief and immediate period of time. Notwithstanding the denial, in reality, when the temporary favorable market trend is followed by recession the business faces adversity causing order volumes from their customers drying up and thereby business is thrown in to financial adversity.

But once again these entrepreneurs resort to blaming the market factors as the prime cause for the adversity rather than the fact that they were wrong in the first place.

## Studying and Learning from Business Success -the summary

Let us now turn to look at the mindset to a different entrepreneurial fraternity and how they understood their business success under a similar set of circumstances as above.

These businesses which interpreted their success realistically observed that the very first time when the success occurred it was not because of the business but the favorable market trend that visited the business. They knew that it was not endorsement of their skillsets or the organization trend or validation of their business strategies or even the endorsement that planning, strategy ,processes are merely time wasting activities.

Similarly, when failure occurred to these businesses they did not allow self-denial and finding another entity to blame as the way to deal with the adverse experience. Instead through their passion for the business they observed and identified 'where they went wrong' and made their lessons from their dispassionate findings. In this way the failure was turned in to an opportunity.

## No second chance -The reality for many Entrepreneurs

Most entrepreneurs are fast learners and are continuously creating the rules and the practices out of their trials and the errors. In doing so, when the failure streaks are repeated, the direct financial impact of ad hoc decisions, lack of planning and processes translate as business losses which are carried forward within their businesses.

Some of these entrepreneurs may not really stand a second chance given that they may have already burnt their entire limited life savings and blemished their personal credibility while in their first entrepreneurial stint. Hence in the first entrepreneurial stint learning from the experience of peers, deeply observing while being dispassionate and nonjudgmental, being patient and composed, and taking guidance from the right advisors, mentors and seniors help entrepreneurs in their entrepreneurial journey to mitigate impairing and irretrievable financial losses and recurring failures from occurring in their businesses.

Intrinsically, it must be borne in mind that businesses are meant to be perpetual entities in other words they are meant to exist for a long period of time with the purpose of creating profit and causing wealth creation while meeting their social commitments.

**The importance of Planning approach while managing business**

Armed with a Vision for the business enterprise every entrepreneur sets up their business and in their forward journey make promises and commitments both to themselves and their stakeholders. And then as they exist and grow they make more promises to the customers and vendors /suppliers the institutional creditors and so on. It is accurate to say that every business is borne out of commitment made by the founder-entrepreneur to the investing capital, the obligations towards the loans providers, the payment towards the operational infrastructure, the payments towards the raw material cost, all of which have to be met on a definitive day on or as per a predetermined timeframe.

With regard to a particular organization, it is abundantly clear that unplanned, arbitrary, chaotic, and segmented actions of the founder management cannot produce outcomes that are predictable in a 'period on period' time frame. Those entrepreneurs who adopt a 'planned approach' to the management of their businesses are able to produce measured outcomes to meet the payment obligations month on month.

So, the salient question that arises here is 'How can the entrepreneur meet these measured fixed financial commitments out of a business whose direction, and control to produce predictable outcomes that is adequate to meet the financial obligations is not entirely in the founder entrepreneurs hands?

Yet, the truth is that businesses exist in an uncertain world. Businesses have to exist by surviving and growing and expressing itself through changing business cycles that form its external reality .Each trade cycle brings new trends and changes and all such changes bring new challenges. But the business has to face the challenges and yet remain strong and resilient. Businesses need to be capable of foreseeing change and then converting the change as the new business opportunity to produce the competing edge for their products and services and as the outcome make it the cause of business success.

Many successful businesses have shown the way by their example of how to grow an entrepreneurial business to become successful and consistently growing from strength to strength. Secondly the way to ensure business success in setting up and running a business by engaging minimal Assets, Meagre capital and limited resources in a highly competitive market place and a tough business environment .

Consciously directing your company in a envisioned, predetermined direction through planning and strategy is meant to produce the business outcome in a consistent and predictable manner. In this way businesses are able to repeat their performance over and over again quarter after quarter with great uniformity and consistency. In this way these businesses are able to accurately predict and deliver the budgeted profitability and the return on investment and become valuable enterprises. Given that they are able to fulfil their commitment to their stakeholders without exposing their stakeholders to the vagaries and uncertainties of changes in the market place. This is true for all businesses whether they are an early stage business that has a 4 person team or a growing organization with a forty member team.

## The relevance of change in management

When we talk about change in the context of business organizations we are really analyzing how external and internal changes influence longevity of businesses? What is the impact of change?

What are the realities of change ? the preparedness of entrepreneurs to accept new truths and new paradigms that change produces ?

As businesses evolve they realize that they have to stay perpetually prepared to deal with change in their external and internal circumstances. It is said that change is the only permanent reality in the world and it is truth that businesses learn to cope with in order to stay relevant surviving and growing all the way.

In one sense, evolution is the constructive word to express the phenomena called change. Businesses realize early enough that in order to successfully manage change they have to be dynamic and vibrant and always be in a state of readiness to alter as and when required every facet of their business from their business purpose or their ethos or their vision, their goals and objectives their business models their products and solutions and so on.

Change brought new technology inventions from which arose new solutions which addressed the customers problem in a different and novel way which made it possible for the customer to experience a new way of doing things. In that sense, businesses are evolving by constructively deploying change to galvanize their growth and ensure survival and become financially relevant in the world. It is pertinent to note that entrepreneurs need to be ready with an open mind to diagnose and observe those aspects which do not serve the interest of their business and quit those practices and adopt new rules and understandings which can lead their business in the path of progress and business growth.

## The Case of Entrepreneurs who resisted change

It is true that 'change as a phenomenon' becomes a challenging event for older established businesses with a substantial vintage, significant market share as they face a different experience while dealing with the reality called 'Change'.In these older businesses, internally predominant number of senior staff members who occupy key management positions in the organization live within their own ideas and dogmas many of which have already been repealed and rewritten by the 'new world order' influencing the field of businesses.

Such 'older businesses' though in one sense benefitted from the 'past wisdom' of its senior team members, at the same time they fail to leverage new ideas and innovations. As they have not adapted with the most current and new technology paradigm they lose the advantage of their 'key value proposition', 'unique product advantages' and even they may gradually lose their 'cost competitiveness' and all the factors would result in a drop in the product brand market share.

**Entrepreneurs who saw change as the next big business opportunity.**

Yet it is true that on the other hand , early enough many entrepreneurs while in their growth trajectory realized the changing rules of the game and so acted proactively and more dynamically. These entrepreneurs were able to quickly metamorphose and catalyze and direct a business transformation in their organization and even create the phenomenon such as the 'caterpillar transforming in to the butterfly' thereby producing a high probability of business success through geometric growth progression hand in hand with business consolidation.

It is aslo true that in the case of older businesses the discussion about change is not limited to the business but also the entrepreneur as he enters in to an 'Older Age profile' in other words as they move from the 'middle age to the senior age' threshold. In case of those businesses which are managed by single founder entrepreneurs, when the founder has attained the status as senior citizens, the businesses suffer and the brand face 'value dilution' as the entrepreneur loses his 'aspiration ,and sometimes loses his passion ,initiative and sense of purpose in the context of the business. Let us discuss the case of older business from one another business dimension that is business succession.

Business Succession

In the case of businesses where the ageing founder do not visualize and put in place a clear succession trajectory and fails to put in place a professional management to grow the business with the same vision and passion the business, the product and the brand loses its value over a period of time.

Many of these entrepreneurs are not able to consider and initiate 'strategic business exit' as a conscious well thought out option to ensure continuity for the business and the brand concerned .They invariably lack the conviction the strength and the vigor to fulfil that important responsibility.

In other words, those senior founder entrepreneurs who were not observant and failed to see the imperatives well in time continued to manage their business without any initiative or true passion and a strong sense of purpose to keep the business going. But these entrepreneurs later realized that during this phase the value of the business was effectively eroded.

And so, for the legal heirs and successors, upon death of the founder entrepreneur the business fetched virtually nothing other than the salvage value of the asset, the brand value, the business reputation and goodwill having been considerably eroded. All this in other words did nothing for creating an 'entrepreneur legacy' for the entrepreneur for having founded and created a great enterprise which was able to create wealth and contribute to social empowerment as end outcome. It is evident for every business in the aforementioned situation the challenge of succession and need for continuity for the business is a subject of great concern. Businesses cannot lose sight of the paradigm and the truth that 'a business is busy growing and if not growing, then it is really busy dying.'

In comparison, a number of more prudent senior entrepreneurs who could foresee the imperative of succession and make their observations and inferences early enough thoughtfully prepared their business for the change in other words the smooth transition of authority and business governance.

Other entrepreneurs planned their strategic exit from their businesses through sale of their equity stake in the company or entered in to merger and acquisition transaction well in time, when the business was performing and derived considerable value for their equity stake.

Through the forgoing, in a concise form some of the important concepts and realities concerning entrepreneurs and their business enterprises have been briefly elucidated for the purpose of introduction in to the entrepreneurs business growth manual. In the succeeding lines and the relevant chapters many of these aspects are discussed in great detail across different chapters for the purpose of clarity.

# CHAPTER TWO

# THE ENTREPRENEUR

This book is for entrepreneurs. So, the natural place to start is by talking about those persons making foray as an entrepreneur and in turn who are in the process of setting up their business enterprise. It would leave no doubt to anyone if we said that the entrepreneur is the most important and the pivotal factor with respect to the enterprise.

To start from basics, the enterprise comes in to being from an initial stage of what could be described best as 'ideation stage'. The person engaged in the process of germinating and evolving the 'seed idea' or the core 'Business idea' which is eventually pursued by the business enterprise, is therefore described as the 'founder' of the particular enterprise.

The so called ' original Idea' potentially evolves through process of ideation in to what could be eventually described as a 'Product' or a 'solution' or a 'Service' 'as case may be' or a combination of all or some of them.

The evolution of the idea is immensely benefited when there is a 'very clear perspective' and 'deep understanding' of the 'problem' that the business is looking to 'address and solve' through the envisaged 'product or solution or service'.

So, let us understand the term problem and the term problem statement through a theoretical explanation of; 'what is a 'problem statement', from the perspective of a business venture.

A problem statement can be said to be the concise description of a problem or challenge that a startup is trying to solve. The problem statement also explores to identify the root cause of the problem and to define the scope of a proposed solution. A problem statement should be specific, measurable, achievable, relevant, and time-bound (SMART). It should also clearly communicate the impact of the problem on the business or target market.

The problem statement is an important and integral part of the entrepreneurial business venture and it helps to focus the efforts of the team on a specific problem and provides a clear target for the solution. It is typically developed as part of the problem discovery and definition phase of the startup process and is used to guide the development of a business plan or product roadmap.

Thus in summary, a problem statement is a crucial element of a startup's overall strategy and helps to ensure that the team is working towards a clear and achievable goal.

Similarly, hand in hand with the realistic understanding of the problem it becomes extremely important for the business to trace and identify the profile of the target entity whether 'individual' or a business ' which is said to be 'facing the problem', in other words 'the one you could call' the real 'Owner of the problem'. This entity or the individual being termed as the target customer.

Thus being the Founder entrepreneur is an 'onerous responsibility', far different from most other responsibilities that a person would have assumed in the course of their material life.

And for most entrepreneurs without Co-founders the journey in the initial period could be a lone struggle often without the availability of a proper team and such persons being left with complex and multiple challenges and having to 'fend for themselves'.

In one sense from a financial perspective depending on their access and availability of capital the entrepreneur will face challenges and will be determined'.

It is also a fact that majority of the ventures being initially 'boot strapped' or in other words 'having not resorted to external capital avenues confined the financing of their business within their limited personal resources.

## Bootstrapping

For the sake of greater clarity we can examine the theoretical meaning of the word bootstrapping as it is construed and understood. Bootstrapping refers to the process of starting and growing a business using personal resources and without outside funding. It involves using personal savings, credit cards, and other forms of debt to finance the business, rather than seeking investment from venture capitalists or other external sources.

Bootstrapping is often associated with startups and small businesses, as it allows entrepreneurs to maintain control over their company and avoid giving up equity to outside investors.

Bootstrapping therefore makes the entrepreneur's journey far more 'daunting' and a 'test of perseverance and tenacity'.

However, it can also be a challenging and risky approach, as it requires the founders to have a strong financial foundation and the ability to generate revenue from the outset.

Bootstrapping can be an effective way to get a business off the ground, especially in the early stages when the business is still in the development phase and may not yet be ready for external investment. It can also be a useful way to assess the viability of a business idea before committing significant resources or seeking external funding. It can be a challenging but potentially rewarding approach for entrepreneurs who are willing to take on the risk and have the financial resources to do so.

Thus, it is paramount for entrepreneurs to handle these moments that makes their 'entrepreneurial journey' most 'productive and meaningful' for the business and their life itself. Thus we come to the real test of their abilities to handle the new role as 'Entrepreneur'.

How well the entrepreneur is able to cope with the 'new found role' awaits to determine the real outcomes they will produce by the end of the first lap of their entrepreneurial journey.

Their capacity to handle the Entrepreneurial role as the 'founder 'would primarily depend on 'who they are' in other words their 'profile' which may include their education, skill, training, experience leadership qualities, personality traits and so on. It is true that if we take the case of a new entrepreneurial venture which is in the process of being set up or being in its early stages the 'qualities of the founder entrepreneur' is likely to influence most of the 'early decision ' of such enterprise 'in the making'.

It is now recognized that managing the enterprise certainly calls for certain distinct attributes and qualities and these have over time come to be recognized as 'preferred entrepreneurial qualities .These attributes are beneficial for entrepreneurs to manage and steer the business on a path to success or in other words the destination called 'Business Goals'.It is also true that every business venture is originally set up by the founder entrepreneur based on their vision with the innate desire to make the venture successful.

A Founder-Entrepreneur's capacity to handle the role will be directly derived from the existence of these entrepreneurial qualities. In other words, 'absence of qualities' could adversely impact their capacity to handle their role as the founder. It is a matter of study that large number of business failures are ultimately traced to the 'entrepreneur himself' in terms the basic question 'whether he entrepreneur founder possessed or lacked basic entrepreneurial attributes.

It is also not in doubt that the entrepreneur who possesses entrepreneurial qualities are better equipped to deal with business adversities and thereby increases the probability of being more able to steer the business to a path of success and thus mitigating the possibility of failure. This means that in ultimate analysis the success or failure of a business is dependent on amongst others, on one important factor and that is 'whether the founder of the entrepreneurial venture has entrepreneurial qualities'.

Yet, it is true that all business ventures are not necessarily started by persons with entrepreneurial qualities. And it may be true that large number of person's engaged in Business may not be even aware of 'imperatives' of possessing these qualities to determine the success of their business.

It becomes necessary to discuss what really are typical entrepreneurial qualities or attributes.

**Entrepreneurial qualities**

Who is an entrepreneur? What are the more identifiable qualities required for an entrepreneur?

Some of the aspects that come to our mind when describing an entrepreneur typically are qualities like leader ship, clarity of vision, passion for the idea or technology, risk taking capacity, growth mindset , belief in team work , aspiration for wealth creation and so on.

The above list is only indicative and there being more qualities and attributes that may be largely identified in entrepreneurs which are the most beneficial to the entrepreneur. Let us sum up the most identifiable and desirable qualities for an entrepreneur as follows:

Passion is perhaps the most important attribute for an entrepreneur. Successful entrepreneurs are often highly passionate about their business idea, the problem that the idea and the solution that is based on the idea is going to solve thus they have a strong belief in the value of their product or service. This passion becomes the source of their perseverance ,determination and resolve to overcome the challenges and setbacks that are common in the early stages of starting a business.

Persistence is another required attribute for an entrepreneur. Entrepreneurs often face many obstacles and setbacks as they work to grow their businesses. Being persistent and determined can help entrepreneurs to overcome these challenges and stay focused on their long-term goals.

Creativity is an important attribute required for entrepreneurs. Entrepreneurs need to think creatively in order to identify opportunities and develop innovative solutions to problems.

The ability to adapt or in other words adaptability and to pivot in response to changing market conditions is crucial for entrepreneurs. Being flexible and open to change can help entrepreneurs to stay ahead of the curve and remain competitive.

Strong communication skills are essential for entrepreneurs, as they need to be able to clearly articulate their vision and persuade others to support their ideas.

Leadership is another important attribute required for entrepreneurs. Successful entrepreneurs have strong leadership skills and the ability to inspire and motivate others.

Risk-taking attribute is essential for entrepreneurs. It is true that entrepreneurship involves taking risks, and the ability to assess and manage risk is crucial for success.

Resourcefulness is a valuable attribute for the entrepreneur. Entrepreneurs need to be resourceful to maximize their limited resources and find creative ways to achieve their goals.

Networking skills namely the capacity to build and maintain relationships with other professionals and potential partners can be crucial for the success of a startup. Strong networking skills can help entrepreneurs to build a supportive network of contacts useful for the business.

Financial management skills will be an invaluable attribute for entrepreneurs. Being able to manage financial resources effectively is crucial for entrepreneurs, as they are often working with limited resources and need to be able to make the most of every unit of investment.

Let us consider the illustration of an entrepreneur who has founded a startup enterprise.

Among the core attributes that the entrepreneur may need to have, we may consider one important attribute which is essentially 'passion for the business'.

Similarly, another attribute from the perspective of a startup enterprise may be 'Innovation' specifically in terms of the entrepreneurs zeal in finding a 'large enough problem' and creating a 'disrupting technology based solution' that solves the customer problem and delivers value to the target customer. In this example through the sale of such a solution to multiple customers the startup driven by the entrepreneur is likely to produce for itself the outcome of higher sales and optimum profit.

As a general reference to other 'potential entrepreneurial traits' the qualities such as the 'aspiration for exponential growth' and 'scalability with an exponential or geometric growth rate' may be an attribute for really ambitious startup entrepreneurs.

'Risk is an integral part' of the startup business, and a startup set up by the entrepreneur who is driven by passion has inherently a higher success rate. With respect to the ownership of the 'Startup business' as compared to 'SME business' it is imperative that startup entrepreneurs need to have a more open perspective about the ownership of the business enterprise.

Organization entity is by itself inanimate by nature and a business becomes successful when the founder entrepreneur is able to bring in all the inputs required for its success. If the necessary and right inputs are not applied because of the limitation of the founder entrepreneur, the business is more likely to fail in achieving its potential and purpose.

In summary, it needs to be emphasized that an entrepreneur with more of the typical entrepreneurial qualities have a high degree and propensity to succeed in the entrepreneurial journey as compared to their peers who were unable to imbibe even the basic traits that the entrepreneurial journey will eventually demand from the entrepreneur by putting the entrepreneur to test during the worst period of adversity.

**Qualities of successful entrepreneurs**

In order to gain larger perspective on the subject of entrepreneur qualities let us look at the qualities of the following well known entrepreneurs who have succeeded in building businesses from small startup business to large businesses which are today unicorns. The entrepreneur founders are Steve Jobs, Bill Gates, Jeff Bezos, Jack Ma, Mark Zuckerberg.

Steve Jobs, Bill Gates, Jeff Bezos, Jack Ma, and Mark Zuckerberg are all highly successful entrepreneurs who have made significant contributions to the technology and business worlds. Each of these individuals has unique qualities and characteristics that have helped them achieve success in their respective fields.

Steve Jobs was known for his innovative and visionary approach to business, as well as his ability to inspire and motivate others. He was also known for his intense focus and attention to detail, which helped him create products that were both aesthetically pleasing and highly functional.

Bill Gates is known for his strong technical skills, particularly in the field of computer programming. He was also known for his business acumen and ability to identify and capitalize on new opportunities.

Jeff Bezos is known for his strategic thinking and ability to identify and pursue long-term opportunities. He has also been praised for his ability to build and scale successful businesses, as well as his focus on customer satisfaction.

Jack Ma is known for his ability to identify and capitalize on new business opportunities in the tech industry. He is also known for his leadership skills and ability to build and manage successful teams.

Mark Zuckerberg is known for his innovative approach to social media and his ability to identify and pursue new opportunities in the tech industry. He is also known for his strong leadership skills and ability to build and manage successful teams.

**Impact of entrepreneurial qualities**

One important question that becomes relevant is :what is the impact of entrepreneurial qualities on the success of the business enterprise?

To get the point through we can we take the example of team Leadership and team work among some of the most important attributes for the founder entrepreneur?

It is observed that large number of entrepreneur founders try to do everything by themselves very seldom choosing not to rely on any other person. In other words the entrepreneur founder is inherently 'not a team player' who does not believe in the virtue of team work or sharing responsibilities or delegating duties by building a team. Such a person can be said to possess a different 'temperament or attribute' that makes them more comfortable performing all important task all by themselves and this may have an adverse influence on their entrepreneurship Role.

Let us take the example of a new business enterprise which is being set up by such a founder entrepreneur.

Such a business organization is more likely to be 'influenced' by this 'particular attribute' of the entrepreneur which in turn causes the business to suffer from 'lack of team work', segmented working style, low productivity, including potential for high attrition of their efficient employees and so on .As the organization grows bigger this situation eventually lead to crisis and could lead to imminent business failure.

Let us analyses the subject of the entrepreneurial attribute of leadership quality and teamwork in a larger perspective and in so far as it impacts the success of the business enterprise.

The term 'Organisation' by natural understanding and definition is inherently the 'aggregation of two or more persons' who come to work together to serve a 'common business idea or purpose' under the leadership of a person or persons called the 'founder or founders' who have started the particular entrepreneurial venture.

So, the core central principle of an organization is therefore about 'teamwork' and 'mutual interdependencies', harnessing 'group synergies' from diverse strengths and 'complimentary' 'skill sets' of individual team members. which in ultimate analysis need to be harmoniously driven through right leadership to produce positive business outcomes.

So, in the above example it is not in doubt that the 'organization in the making' is likely to suffer in terms of not being able to succeed simply because the founder entrepreneur produced an 'influence' on the business that was 'adverse to team work'.

In final analysis this may evidently lead the business to 'imminent adversity' in terms of the organization being unable to achieve its true business potential.

It is evident therefore that the first rule for success of a business enterprise is that the entrepreneur founder should possess qualities that are called 'entrepreneur qualities' in which the founder entrepreneur and the team's belief in 'team work' the important entrepreneurial trait is a very important aspect.

Through the above we have taken one example of 'team work' to illustrate the point regarding entrepreneurial qualities. Through the succeeding pages, we will explore the subject of entrepreneurial qualities in greater detail by bringing other perspectives .

It is pertinent to note that every entrepreneur needs to necessarily understand the qualities required of the entrepreneur and practice them in so far as it concerns his role as the founder of the organization holding the responsibility to lead the organization to envisaged business and financial outcomes.

In the preceding page, we have already presented the entrepreneurial qualities of five successful founder entrepreneurs namely Bill gates, Mark Zuckerberg, Steve Jobs, Jack Ma, Jeff Bezos. For clarity it may serve the discussion to understand how their entrepreneur qualities have contributed to their business success.

Bill Gates: Bill Gates is known for his passion for technology, persistence, and leadership. He was a strong leader and visionary who was able to develop and execute a long-term strategy for Microsoft. He was also persistent and determined, and was able to overcome setbacks and challenges as he built Microsoft into a global technology leader.

Mark Zuckerberg: Mark Zuckerberg is known for his creativity, adaptability, and communication skills. He was able to identify a need for social networking and develop a solution that quickly gained widespread adoption. He has also been able to adapt to changing market conditions and has effectively communicated the vision and value of Facebook to users and investors.

Steve Jobs: Steve Jobs was known for his passion, creativity, and leadership. He was a visionary who was able to develop innovative products and services that changed the way people live and work. He was also a strong leader who was able to inspire and motivate others to achieve his vision for Apple.

Jack Ma: Jack Ma is known for his creativity, adaptability, and leadership. He was able to identify a need for an online marketplace in China and develop a solution that quickly gained widespread adoption. He has also been able to adapt to changing market conditions and has effectively led Alibaba through its growth and expansion.

Jeff Bezos: Jeff Bezos is known for his persistence, adaptability, and leadership. He was able to identify an opportunity in the online retail market and develop a solution that quickly gained widespread adoption. He has also been able to adapt to changing market conditions and has effectively led Amazon through its growth and expansion. He is also known for his persistence, as he has been able to overcome numerous challenges and setbacks as he has built Amazon into a global e-commerce leader.

Let us turn our attention to a relevant question namely 'what is the difference between Business man and entrepreneur'?

The fact is that every person who is engaged as a founder in setting up or managing a business is not necessarily an 'entrepreneur'. Ideally only those persons in business who possess entrepreneurial qualities can be termed as entrepreneurs.

Ideally, it may be correct to say that every entrepreneur may be a person engaged in running a business. In a sense every entrepreneur is hence a 'business person'.

But every 'Business person' cannot be called an 'entrepreneur'.Hence the term business person as it is termed and used here in the course of this discussion must be understood as 'those business persons' who are 'not entrepreneurs'.

Ideally such 'business persons' fundamentally with a trading mindset are more likely to possess some or all the qualities that are in contrast with the attributes that we have described earlier as important 'entrepreneurial qualities'.

These qualities may be Limited Risk taking capacity, Restricted growth aspiration, more preference for business growth with consolidation, dependence of the business solely on the founders proprietor for capital, more focus on tangible net worth, Asset centric approaches, lack of value in 'wealth creation' approach through 'intangible asset' and so on.

As evident from the above these qualities run in sharp contrast and opposite of the attributes cited under 'desirable entrepreneurial qualities'.

It is thus evident that there is a clear contrast and distinction in mindsets of 'entrepreneurs' and 'business person' in trading businesses. This places entrepreneurs and business persons in two different poles, virtually opposite to one another.

In order to understand startup and their distinction from SMB businesses let us look at the attributes of startups that distinguish startups from other types of businesses:

Innovation: Startups often focus on developing innovative products or solution that uniquely address a large problem which has a sizeable customer base and demand and huge scalability.

Focus on exponential growth in Sales and number of customers is an integral part of the vision and goal of most startups and the rate of growth envisaged is invariably exponentially in Sales Revenues and new customer acquisition.

Adaptability and Agility : At the inception stage generally startups are often lean and agile, mostly not asset intensive, and are started with a small team of employees and bootstrapped are able to quickly and dynamically adapt to changing market conditions formulate new business models, customer acquisition strategies.

High risk: Inherently start up entrepreneurs and investors have a higher risk appetite and they have clarity regarding the Risk Versus Return equation. This aspect makes the startup entrepreneur stand out in comparison with the conventional SME undertaking where the entrepreneur has a lower risk-taking ability.

Potential for high reward: Despite the risks, the potential rewards for startups can be high. Successful startups have the potential to grow rapidly and generate significant profits for their founders and investors.

Let us look at the common understanding of the term Industrialist? is there a distinction between the term 'industrialist' and 'Businessman'.

The view is that 'entrepreneurs' who evolve and grow the businesses largely focusing on setting up Industrial undertakings with a long term perspective may be termed as 'Industrialist' and in that sense there is an accepted distinction between 'business persons' with trading approach and 'Industrialist'.

Can a business person who is setting up a new entrepreneurial venture transform and imbibe the qualities of an entrepreneur at some point in time?

There are large number of successful entrepreneurs who were once business persons pushing traditional model of trading businesses and later transformed themselves to become successful entrepreneurs in their new entrepreneurial foray.

# CHAPTER THREE

# ENTREPRENEURIAL QUALITIES

What is the Linkage between Business Growth and entrepreneurial qualities?

It is not in doubt that among 'entrepreneurial qualities' one specific attribute that stands out is the 'growth mindset' or the vision to create a 'scalable business'.

The growth mindset fuels a different type of determination and passion for the entrepreneur which directly reflect on the business. It is observed that invariably such businesses engage the 'most distinctive and innovative' technologies completely aligning to the customer needs and even have a 'disruptive impact' in the market place as their key differentiator and USP to drive the engine of business growth.

Does the background or the origin of the person impact his capacity to acquire or have entrepreneurial qualities?

In the discussion about the current 'attributes and qualities' possessed by entrepreneurs the important aspect undoubtedly is in terms of 'who these individuals were' prior to starting their entrepreneurial venture.

It is not in doubt that the traits demonstrated by them while managing their current role as entrepreneur in charge of the new business venture, are invariably influenced by their 'origin' or their past background, experience and exposure.

In other words, it is evident that in the course of the earlier occupational stint they have acquired various qualities and traits which have become part of their mental outlook and temperament.

These traits may exert certain influence on their decision making in the later period after the person concerned has assumed the stint as the founder entrepreneur. As an illustration, If the person concerned was an employee in a particular organization prior to his current stint as entrepreneur they may demonstrate the traits during his entrepreneurship particularly the traits that they imbibed in the course of his employment.

This takes us to an interesting question namely based on past background how many types of entrepreneurs can be distinctly identified?

Based on past background , we may be able to identify and categorize entrepreneurs in five different classes namely entrepreneurs who moved from: (a)Educational Campus to entrepreneurship, (b)Businessman to entrepreneur(c)Employment to entrepreneurship(d)Profession to entrepreneurship(e)Home maker to entrepreneurship.

From the above categories, if we take one example of an entrepreneur who was previously an independent professional practicing a certain vocation, it is observed that these people are more likely to demonstrate qualities of past 'professional life' traits particularly those distinctive traits and attributes in their 'current new stint' as an 'entrepreneur' whether it is about handling 'day to day' matters or those requiring 'decision making'. and therefore these individuals are potentially most likely to take longer time in their transformational journey to becoming entrepreneurs.

Similarly, if we take the example of people who were previously in employment prior to their stint as entrepreneur, they are more likely to bring different traits and attitudes which are generally considered typical 'employee mindset' during their current stint with entrepreneurship.

In the succeeding lines we will examine some salient questions like: why origin of entrepreneur is important for 'business success' irrespective of 'whether the transformation is from professional to entrepreneur'? or 'Business person to entrepreneur'? or employment to entrepreneur? or Campus to entrepreneur? as the case may be.

Secondly, in order to succeed in Entrepreneurship should the incumbent entrepreneur shed all the past attributes from the past life which are inconsistent with his new stint in entrepreneurship? whether the new qualities that are consistent with the entrepreneurial life must be cultivated and imbibed in soul and spirit?

**Transformation of professional to entrepreneur -illustration**

To examine all the above questions, we may discuss a very basic illustration to examine the transition of a professional and examine the subject in detail.

A professional footballer at the peak of his career in terms of recognition and great financial accomplishments decided to take the plunge to set up an entrepreneurial venture in the field of 'Organizing Sports events' and 'Celebrity management' and an immediate plan to constitute or own a Football team. As a 'master footballer' who the world respected and emulated his current aspiration was to be the founder of the world's best team.

In the process of setting up the team, without his own knowledge he was slowly becoming a business owner who had to have entrepreneurial traits to attain the aspiration of becoming the world best football team.

Throughout his professional career as an ace footballer he had a huge reputation and brand value with saleability that ensured a disproportionately large financial compensation for him.

The foray in to entrepreneurship proved a difficult challenge for the footballer, far greater than what was expected by him. He had to imbibe new skills that he did not possess. The new entrepreneurial stint required him to be persuasive, more patient , more understanding and well-tempered.

He had no selling skills as he did not need to market himself in the past. In his current stint he had to present his venture to potential players and professionals in a bid to persuade them to join the team and his entrepreneurial venture.

The professional footballer had to fix remuneration for his team members, and unlike in his past life, now as an entrepreneur, he had to be content with being paid from profits, if any.

In order to fund the entrepreneurial venture he had to borrow money to finance the capital to set up the team unlike in his past life when he had no debt liabilities.

It is becoming evident from the above illustration that irrespective of the prior background of the entrepreneur whether a successful professional star in their earlier stint or an ex-employee who was highly successful in their earlier stint in employment, in their foray in to entrepreneurship by setting up an entrepreneurial venture, in order for them to be able to lead the business to path of success they will need to imbibe and come to possess the required entrepreneurial qualities. While doing so, they may need to shed those qualities and temperament that is inconsistent with their new role.

This in turn could become the key determinant of their eventual success in their stint with entrepreneurship. On the contrary If they are unable to realign and imbibe the desirable entrepreneurial qualities in reasonable time, they may fail to lead venture the path to success.

**Transformation of professional to entrepreneur -illustration**

In order to reemphasize the point, let us examine another illustration

An architect in independent practice in his own name identified growth opportunities terms of addressing bigger client accounts and moving in to a total solutions provider status and thus achieving manifold increase in project values, income and profitability.

For this purpose, it was not enough to present the conventional proprietary firm that stood in the Architect's personal name as they realized that bigger and potential new clients look forward to an organization. Thus it became necessary to present an organization with a multifaceted team, team hierarchy, required departments and relevant skill sets. capable of handling the assignment on a turn key basis or end to end basis .

In other words, the Architect realized that new business opportunities are not available to them in their individual capacity. Larger clients and bigger contracts are accessible only when they are able to present a well constituted organization with a competent team of resources, structured policies , robust processes and systems in other words all of which provide an assurance of long term reliability for customers and thereby business perpetuity.

Having set out in this new path the same former proprietary business of the Architect was brought under a new entity with a renewed branding name and style. Internally the team was restructured and reconstituted with new team members having been hired and placed in different job positions. Aligning to this new business initiative a new office set up with necessary infrastructure was created to accommodate the new team and create the right client perception. Thus the business was carried forward in the new business name instead of his independent proprietary name as in the past.

At the end of the relevant financial year when the financial statements of the newly constituted organization was reviewed it was found that though there was increase in operations and incomes in real terms the expenditure had increased and there was net loss in other words expenditure was more than income.

There were limited number of additional jobs and new clients and new business acquired had not radically increased. The Architect is now confused, with the question : what went wrong? was the decision to transform in to an entrepreneur itself erroneous ?

**We may examine the observations and inferences in seriatim:**

The professional turned entrepreneur had created a new organization under a new name and brand name by hiring appropriate people with the 'Right profile and Skill-set' to align with the targeted business opportunity and acquisition of larger customers. The professional sourced capital and further debt funding from bank for meeting the expenses generally as working capital. Though the professional had taken all the major steps in his foray in to entrepreneurship, they failed to do the following:

Entrepreneur was yet to really transform from professional to entrepreneur having failed to imbibe critical entrepreneurial qualities and the true spirit of entrepreneurship.

As the Architect founder who lacked leadership skills, and also had a limited risk taking approach, he did not have an entrepreneurial perspective while taking key decisions in the stint as an entrepreneur.

Though they appointed competent resources who were retained on high salaries he failed to provide right balanced leadership and thereby get their commitment to the business.

There was no internal processes and lack of proper team hierarchy hence even after appointing more resources incurring higher cost due to lack of team work within the team members resulting in lack of direction and wastage of resources.

Decision making was always centralized at the Founder level and there were delays in decisions and approvals thereby affecting access to new business opportunities.

The team was unable to perceive the existence of a brand or a corporate organization that had the potential to grow bigger and offer career prospects professional exposure financial enrichment or even job security.

Instead most of the team members felt that they were working for the Architect in his personal capacity. Those team members who aspired to work in a stable organization were disillusioned.

What was the impact? Most of the able team members realized that given the factors causing the limitation, the particular new organization may not transform into a large organization.

The business suffered because of high degree of employee attrition, with some groups of employees even acting in concert and exiting the business having taken away customers and business opportunities.

The Architect blamed the employees who left him terming them as 'not loyal' while failing to notice what really went wrong? and how his actions could have caused the actions of his erstwhile team members? In this denial he failed to gather the important pieces of wisdom which could 'failure proof' his business in the future stint in business.

In this way the founder could not leverage the brand or the team to acquire business or increase the income in a productive manner and at the same time had to arrange funding for the losses incurred.

In a realistic analysis many traditionally minded professionals lack risk taking capacity and particularly have a low risk appetite. This lack of risk taking approach affect them to attain their ambitions and aspiration to become bigger through their setting up a business and getting in to the shoes of an entrepreneur.

Due to their past experience as an independent practitioner they continue to be rather constricted in their outlook and perspective about professional opportunities. Inherently these professionals tend to be individualistic ,self-driven, professionally insecure, and even after they move to in to the new role they are unwilling to change or transform.

Many of them do not have the right leadership skills to build an enterprise which would call for team creation with perseverance and tenacity while seeing the big growth potential for value creation and recognition .

For a deeper understanding we may consider a third example as follows:

**Transformation of professional to entrepreneur -illustration**

A famous cardiologist in a metropolitan city who was at the peak of his career with substantial earnings had a strong vision to set up a large multispecialty hospital with the latest technology, state of the art equipment's and to be managed by professionals from multiple specialties.

The doctor embarked on the entrepreneurial journey of creation of a large healthcare organization by sourcing huge capital, investments, debt funding. The organization also went on to hire experienced doctors and able support staff by identifying and hiring them from other existing hospitals to join the new enterprise that he created.

The doctor realized that in order to lead his business venture needed to understand the business aspects and imbibe entrepreneurial qualities which would help him to build a complete organization which he may be able to manage successfully.

The doctor also realized early enough that while acquiring new qualities they also had to do away with certain traits and temperaments that are not consistent with the new role as entrepreneur. Thus, all of the above aspects collectively called for a major transformation of his temperament and thinking.

The challenges provided by this need for transformation was indeed daunting for the doctor for many reasons.

As an independent practicing professional, they did not have to create an organization, nor did they have to share the financial benefit that they receive in lieu of the services rendered to their patients with any other person or an organization. Further, their leadership qualities were never put to test. Their entire financial aspirations were being met though their individual skills and their own professional competence and acumen. They did not have to bear any particular type of Risk in their professional work that they could not otherwise manage and could remain individualistic, self-centric, self-reliant and so on.

In the new found role as founder entrepreneur their skill as a professional cardiologist was effectively over shadowed by the need to acquire newer entrepreneur and business skills in order to set up, manage the business enterprise and eventually lead the venture to success.

Further as entrepreneur they had to take risk, invest capital in the process of building an organization by creating a team and providing leadership to the team. In this manner transformation to an entrepreneur became the key for their success in the entrepreneurial venture.

In this particular case, though the doctor invested on infrastructure and technology and state of the art equipment having mobilized capital and debt liabilities for the venture, he could not mobilize doctors, create the right team, provide effective leadership, install confidence in the team and provide the right branding and visibility for the venture.

His personality as an independent professional dominated his actions which were in complete non alignment with his role as head of the entrepreneurial business. This eventually caused the professional doctor to fail in his entrepreneurial journey.

Let us now discuss another category of entrepreneurs namely 'technicians' by addressing the question :

**Transformation - Technician to an Entrepreneur**

What are the real challenges in the transformation of the Technician to an Entrepreneur?

Large number of founder entrepreneurs of SMB Businesses in their previous stint have been technicians or technocrats .These persons are technically qualified and experienced in a particular knowledge or 'industry sphere' however they may have limited perspective with regard to commercial and business matters and may lack even a basic concept regarding setting up or managing a business.

Their understanding about setting up and running a business may be limited to their understanding about procuring and installing the manufacturing machines and thereafter carrying out the production activity.

They may pay limited attention to other non-technical matters .In this manner business, commercial and financial spheres may be largely trivialized and overlooked. The principle that business success outcome can be produced only by harmonizing technical competence holistically with the commercial and business management aspects may not be understood at all.

In this manner many technician turned entrepreneurs start their entrepreneurial venture with a trivial and simplistic understanding of the non-technical commercial business matters investing their hard earned savings and loan funds raised from other sources .They may be often oblivious of the need to upgrade their own knowledge and understanding even while relying on others team members or third party consultants , advisors or mentors who could guide them through the process.

To illustrate many of these businesses run by entrepreneurs who are previously competent technicians or technocrats churn out technically perfect products using the most sophisticated and well organized technical facilities. But yet they fail commercially as they are unable to sell their products or find enough paying customers.

These entrepreneurs inherently being less aware about the business side as compared to the technical side are constrained to go through the process of trial and error while taking business decisions. Many of these businesses become cash strapped with cash losses because the entrepreneur were not able to financially manage their business whether in terms of profitability or working capital management or other commercial matters.

Those mistakes which have larger financial implication thereby result in wiping out the entire capital and the debts remaining unpaid. These situations become imminent when the incidence of adverse loss creating causes remain unaddressed by the entrepreneur and therefore compounded. These situations can potentially cause the failure of the business.

Many of the technicians being inherently competent in their sphere of activity may attempt to do all the work all by themselves delegating the least by creating a competent team. They may lack the invaluable quality required for the entrepreneur which is team work.

They may lack the perspective or the vision that make the businesses grow commercially. Often their understanding may be limited to technical aspects may be like production quantity and so on while having blind spot on every other thing.

As they may lack a business perspective, they may be oblivious to the need for creating an organization and team within that organization in order to create scale in operations, achieve sales and profitability.

Thus when the product or the solution created or invented by them become successful and accepted by the end customer seeking more volumes besides potential to add many new customers they are unable to scale their business to address the long awaited opportunity.

Many technician turned entrepreneur remain overwhelmed and preoccupied with the technical details and this may cause them to overlook the grander vision , the larger business purpose ,Revenue goals and profitability goals, all of which lead to the condition best explained by the phrase ' missing the woods for the trees'.

Many of these technician turned entrepreneurs may inherently lack people management skills and leadership skills which are paramount quality for their success in their stint as an entrepreneur.

It is also observed that for many technicians their passion for the business may be limited to the technical aspects of their business rather than a holistic view of the product solution and the business in its entirety.

Technical person may risk averse or in other words they may not have a high degree of risk-taking capacity which is a quality required for an entrepreneur. This may spring from a rather limited idea or exposure to business and financial matters and the commercial aspects of managing a business. This may lead them to different contradictions from time to time while in their entrepreneurial stint. They may be indecisive in their handling the affairs of the business which could hurt the business. They may harbor aspirations about various aspects of their business but may fail to implement the same completely. This may in turn cause loss of capital and eventual business failure.

**The challenges for Transformation -employee to entrepreneur**

What are the real challenges in the transformation of the employee to an Entrepreneur?

Yet another class of entrepreneurs are those who went through the stint as an employee in an organization or more than one organization prior to becoming an entrepreneur.

Inherently Persons who started their occupational life as an employee in an organization by nature may have many traits which could be the reason for choosing employment as compared to other career options. Yet there are many persons who chose employment as compared to entrepreneurship largely for financial reasons and ensuring economic support and financial security for their families.

In any case in the course of their employment they are more likely to imbibe and acquire certain qualities and traits that ultimately influence their individual personality and outlook in life in subsequent years.

In order to illustrate we may take the example of some typical traits that many employees of organization may possess under normal circumstances. As employee they have limited self-initiative, they are used to another person normally a person more senior to them taking decisions or assuming the accountability and the responsibility, exposing themselves to risk or handling the planning, coordinating, and controlling the task or the project concerned. The employee being part of a balanced team hierarchy may be confined to accomplish the task assigned within the entire department workflow and job output.

In this way those who were previously employees in larger organizations are more likely to have exposure working in compartmentalized department environments which primarily offer lesser and more limited experience with least possibility for diversity.

Thus many of them may have constricted competence and limited exposure to handling risk and uncertainties. adverse circumstances and surprises.

If we take the case of entrepreneur who were previously employees who have held managerial positions and in employment for a longer period depending on the level in their previous organization they may have enjoyed powers and facilities, assigned with a competent team to assist them, all infrastructure being provided to them with ample financial powers and financial budget being available to them while handling large project outlays. Invariably this type of experience influence their personality traits.

Similarly, by nature, many of these individuals may have limited or lower tolerance to handling adversity. Many of these individuals are likely to be more inflexible and not easily integrating with others in the organization, in other words they tend to be 'not effective team players'.

In their subsequent stint as an entrepreneur, for the above individuals everything changes and they may need to handle 'shoe string' budgets, and deal with limited financial resources, all of which may become a necessity while handling entrepreneurial responsibilities.

Unlike in the case of their previous tenure in employment, in their subsequent entrepreneurial stint they may have to handle the crisis all by themselves .They may not have the luxury of team or a senior person to handle the line of fire, they may have to single handedly lead the business through the period of adversities. How they are able to handle the crisis would depend on how soon they are able to metamorphose and transform in to the entrepreneur and imbibe the qualities that would galvanize the entrepreneur to handle the challenges placed by the new role.

It is being clarified that there is no generality with respect to any of the aspects aforementioned and there is no generalized rule in other words there are large number of exceptions.

In reality, a large number of entrepreneurs who were previously employees have quickly transformed in the course of their entrepreneurial journey and effortlessly embraced their new role. They imbibed and demonstrated the entrepreneurial traits even within a limited period of time. In this way they empowered themselves to effectively increase the probability of achieving success in their entrepreneurial business and to be able to produce high performing businesses.

Through the foregoing there is ample clarity with regard to more desirable entrepreneurial qualities for the success of the entrepreneur venture.

**Case about Entrepreneurs who were previously in trading businesses**

Let us turn our attention to discuss the transformation of many individuals who were previously business persons running trading businesses, shops, family style businesses and so on in to entrepreneurs.

Evidently, these persons are likely to demonstrate number of qualities that they have imbibed in the course of their stint in handling trading business. For instance these persons are more likely to prefer individual centric enterprises. They may possess Limited risk taking ability, in turn being very risk averse. They may not possess long term perspective on leader ship or even consider importance of organizational team building or even Team skill development. They may have limited belief in participative management style. They may possess inclination to hire one or two persons as super managers with a low financial budget to meet the end goal. They may possess the least or limited belief in planning and strategy and Profit and cash on hand is considered wealth with limited perspective on intangible value creation.

It is evident that in their journey as entrepreneur some or all of the above qualities may cause adversity for the entrepreneurial business.

Many business persons embark on the entrepreneurial journey after being inspired and encouraged by the 'success of entrepreneurs' and the growth opportunities that the avenue offers to individuals with aspiration. While making their foray in to entrepreneurship, many such business persons tend to set up new entrepreneurial ventures while some of them join as partner or associate with existing entrepreneurial ventures already in existence. This association with the organization may be in the nature of a 'general partner' or a 'financial partner' or a 'strategic business partner'. Even after taking up such a role it is a possibility that they may not have truly understood the core difference in traits between an 'entrepreneur' and the 'typical business man'.

As an illustration let us consider the essential entrepreneurial quality namely 'risk taking capacity' and analyze the 'perspective' of business persons while dealing with decisions involving 'risk' in their new business association with entrepreneurs as 'partner' in the particular business establishment.

Such businesspersons who are currently in their entrepreneurial stint as partner continue to possess the attribute of being 'deeply risk averse'. In the course of their managing their new role in the business covering both strategic business matters or financial or routine day to day matters this may impact and apply to all the matters at the critical moment of decision making.

At the time of taking critical business decisions with financial implication if we consider the example of a decision regarding capital infusion into the business or taking exposure to additional loans proposed to be borrowed from banks or creating assets , or acquiring infrastructure for the business or scaling the business revenues by higher marketing spend or appointing competent people on high salary and emoluments and so on , the person may become completely indecisive and procrastinate taking critical decisions. This level of indecisiveness may potentially paralyze the business and thereby produce adversity and loss for the business.

If we take the example of a business in a 'high growth technology' related field, It is possible that such a person with a 'low risk appetite' may 'shy away' from the critical decision with regard to Research and Development and innovation and even possibly limit the 'product innovation budgets' thereby jeopardizing the 'true intrinsic potential' of the business.

In this way as they come from the place of 'risk averse', these persons may not have a high aspiration for business growth. In their current stint as an 'entrepreneur', this attitude could be limiting factor in their efforts to achieve strategic business goals for their entrepreneurial venture .

Let us take another example of a business man who made a foray in to entrepreneurship by joining an existing entrepreneurial venture by being inducted as 'Cofounder' along with existing partner founders being entrepreneurs who possess entrepreneurial qualities .

In this case if the business person is not able to transform and imbibe the spirit of entrepreneurship there is a high chance for certain differences and conflicts to arise within the founder management team which may adversely affect the business.

When such persons become part of the board of directors of such a Business while the board of directors of such an entity is considering critical business matters that have financial implication as Such persons being previously 'business person' with a limited interpretation regarding Risk may adversely impact the business decision that could be critical and beneficial for the business.

Thus it is amply clear that the business person being inherently highly risk averse, their indecisiveness may affect the nature of the decision making and lead to delayed decisions and longer response time for Board approvals and corporate decision all of which may adversely affect the business.

Businesses person being least appreciative of participative decision making and the advantage of consensus approach while taking major decisions are likely to cause conflicts within the board. While they may not integrate with the team, on the contrary they may even create an informal organization of their loyalists within the organization. In some cases, they may attempt to take tacit control of the affairs of the business and all of which may potentially draw the business in different conflicting directions.

In order to consolidate our understanding let us take the example of Business which is constituted as partnership entities with partners and co-founders from different past backgrounds and address the question namely:

**Entrepreneurs with Different backgrounds as Co-founders**

What is the impact of entrepreneurs with different background coming together as partners or co-founders in the same business establishment?

In an establishment where there are founders from different backgrounds where, for example, one founder was an employee in their earlier stint and another a professional in independent practice in their earlier stint, evidently these individuals are likely to demonstrate distinct traits as a consequence of their past. Whether these experiences help or hurt the establishment would however depend on the transformation that they have been able to achieve after they assume the role in entrepreneurship.

It is true that when there is unity of purpose and great deal of cooperation and compatibility as between the partners regarding the business direction that the vision for the business , there is greater probability of the business achieving commercial success .

On the contrary, when there is lack of cooperation, lack of unity and limited understanding between the partners the team members are likely to be disillusioned thereby causing conflict within the team members .This in turn may lead to the same impact percolating downwards to the team and causing conflict within the team and poor team work. Thus the business will have a segmented and disillusioned team who will not be able to work in a common direction and meet its goals. This situation is capable of creating loss and business failure.

As an illustration, we may take the example of one of the software company which was set up by three persons of which two of whom have directly moved from the tech incubation facility in their alumni directly to setting up a business .whereas the third partner actually had prior experience having run a business establishment in the past. Having started the entrepreneurial venture, over the next three-year period even though the business succeeded in building an 'enterprise - software' product which was accepted by reputed customers, the business failed in being able to market or sell the product .This ultimately lead to the business being unable to sustain the cost and thereby incurred cash losses.

In hindsight, the reason for the losses and failure was traced to the lack of entrepreneurial spirit on the part of the partner entrepreneur concerned in terms of effectively failing to cooperate and work as a team to take the business in one unified direction. There was lack of process, systems and policies leading to segmented decision making, lack of harmony within the team members all of which resulted in misdirection of the business and cash losses.

It is true that in businesses with more than one founders from diverse backgrounds such as employment background or business background or campus background having succeeded in total transformation, if they can collectively work as a cohesive team and create the right synergies using their respective strength to complement each other and to the best advantage of the organization, they will be able to lead the business to become extraordinarily successful entities.

In this illustration transformation of the founding person from their previous background to become 'true entrepreneur' will be the key aspect which determine 'success' of their enterprise.

The commitment and passion for their business must ensure willingness of the founders to test and reexamine the relevance of their past knowledge and relearn and up skill as necessary to be able to contribute to their newly assigned role. To put it more precisely, successful entrepreneurs realized the need to reexamine their past knowledge with current realities and new beliefs, ideas and latent knowledge and those that do not serve or have become irrelevant need to necessarily substituted by newer idea and information.

We have discussed the challenge faced by founder entrepreneurs in handling their dual role namely on the one hand - the role as the business functionary such as a CEO or COO or general manager or operational in charge of the business and on the other hand the role of the Investor of capital that they have infused in to their business from their savings or assets or their personal resources. The perspective that an investor brings on the table at the time of a critical business decision could be potentially different from the perspective that is brought by the functionary in the business handling the day-to-day management responsibilities. The founder entrepreneur's ability to handle the different roles while bringing an equilibrium and balance will contribute to the success of the business and vice versa.

**Reasons for Failure attributable to an entrepreneur's qualities**

Let us sum up our understanding by addressing the following question: what are the failure reasons that are directly attributable to the qualities of entrepreneurs ? Some of these reasons may include:

Lack of experience: Entrepreneurs who are new to the business world may lack the necessary knowledge and skills to successfully operate a business. This can lead to a lack of success and ultimately, failure.

Poor decision-making: Entrepreneurs who make poor business decisions, lack of prudent spending without financial checks and balances, indiscriminate approach to taking risk, or not adequately researching the market, may contribute to the failure of their business.

Lack of planning and focus: Entrepreneurs who lack a clear vision or direction for their business may struggle to succeed. This can lead to a lack of focus and a spread of resources too thin, resulting in a lack of progress or success.

Lack of adaptability: Entrepreneurs who are unable to adapt to changing market conditions or consumer demands may struggle to keep their business afloat. This could be due to a lack of innovation or a failure to stay current with industry trends.

Poor leadership: Entrepreneurs who are not effective leaders may struggle to guide their organization and make strategic decisions. This can lead to a lack of direction and a decline in performance.

Lack of motivation: Entrepreneurs who lack motivation or commitment to their business may not put in the necessary effort to succeed. This can lead to a lack of progress and ultimately, failure.

Lack of a support system: Entrepreneurs who do not have a strong support system, such as a mentor or a network of advisors, may struggle to overcome challenges and succeed in the business world.

Besides the above certain attributes like Lack of positive temperament and attitude may limit the capacity of the entrepreneur to build a team. Similarly, limited capacity to take risk could be an impediment for business growth and also may lead to slow decision making and loss of opportunities. Lack of passion for the business may limit the commitment and the power of perseverance of the entrepreneur to succeed in the entrepreneurial stint . Lack of growth appetite may cause the business to lose out to competition and may also eventually cause the business and its brand to be substituted by the competitor in the particular market and which may lead to imminent losses.

Having understood in detail the determinants of success in Entrepreneurship the important question that would engage the mind of every entrepreneur would be how can entrepreneurs imbibe the qualities and overcome the limitations that cause them to fail.

**Overcoming Limitations**

How can entrepreneurs overcome the limitations of not possessing the right skill, relevant knowledge and acquire the desired and useful entrepreneurial qualities to become successful?

Entrepreneurs can break the limitations of not possessing entrepreneurial knowledge and qualities by taking the following initiatives:

Seek out educational resources: There are many resources available to help entrepreneurs learn the skills and knowledge they need to be successful. This can include online courses, workshops, and business education programs.

Surround yourself with successful entrepreneurs: Working with or learning from successful entrepreneurs can be a great way to gain valuable insights and knowledge. Consider joining an industry association or a business incubator or accelerator program or finding a mentor or advisor who can guide you through the entrepreneurial process.

Take calculated risks: Entrepreneurship often involves taking risks, and while it's important to be cautious, sometimes taking calculated risks can lead to new opportunities and growth.

Learn from your mistakes: It is important to embrace failure and learn from mistakes. Every mistake is an opportunity to learn and grow as an entrepreneur.

Stay focused and persistent: Building a successful business takes time and hard work. It's important to stay focused on your goals and persevere through challenges.

Overall, the key to becoming a successful entrepreneur is to continuously learn and grow, and to be willing to take risks and learn from your mistakes.

**Stages in the Entrepreneurial life cycle**

What are the Stages in Entrepreneurial life cycle?

While describing and understanding the origin and the growth of a business tracing the growth stages become paramount. There are different terms that are used to describe the stage of growth of the business venture.

In this way different nomenclature have evolved to represent the stage like Ideation stage, Seed stage, business set up stage , growth stage and so on.

The nomenclature used to represent the stage cover the concept and the idea generation phase, and in a step by manner move to the product prototype or minimum viable product stage, proof of concept stage, product launch stage, business stabilization phase, business growth phase, and so on. If the business goes through a period of stress then it is described as stressed business stage.

In reality each and every stage denote a certain stage of growth in other words a growth threshold that is distinct and specific in terms of the physical condition of the business and the progress achieved till that date.

From a different perspective if we consider the 'current purpose' that a particular business may be pursuing, we can categorize and arrive at broadly three types of businesses namely : Business venture looking to set up their business, secondly Business venture in a growth phase looking to grow bigger and thirdly businesses which are failing and looking to revive and resurrect

**Importance of recognizing stages in Business life cycle**

Why is it necessary to recognize the importance of analyzing and understanding the stages within the entrepreneur-business life cycle?

Will the type of challenges faced by a business change with every passing stage such as early stage and growth stage?

It is true that in the course of their entrepreneurial journey as entrepreneurs and as their businesses evolve, grow and pass through the above critical and distinct stages of the 'business life cycle', entrepreneurs face more diverse, different and new types of challenges on the arrival of every new stage largely arising on account of the business growth attained by them. In summary the type of challenges will directly correlate with the specific stage of the particular business. A business in the seed stage will face a different type of challenge as compared with the business in its growth stage.

It is amply clear that as businesses evolve and traverse through its different growth stages or growth thresholds, entrepreneurs need to recognize to observe and examine the new challenges closely and prepare the organization to cope with the pain points, and threats posed by them without ignoring the potential business opportunities likely to arise at every new growth stage.

In the transformational journey of their business they must reinvent and upgrade their businesses necessarily by induction of competent management and team resources, incorporate new technologies and innovation, processes and automation while strengthening the organization framework in totality. Entrepreneurs also need to revisit and upgrade their understanding and ideas, temperaments and attitudes, acquire new skill sets and knowledge so that they are fully geared to play a pivotal role in the business growth .

At the same time, the founder entrepreneurs may need to be cautious of the fact that they do not become the 'limitation for further growth of their business' while it attains the 'higher threshold of business growth' on the way to become an even larger business entity.

To further understand the importance of recognizing the stage of a business in its business life cycle we may take the case of a business in its growth stage.

The particular business in our illustration has currently a spectacular 'revenue growth trajectory' and 'exponential customer acquisition track record'.This in turn being driven largely by an 'innovative product or solution' and the overall growth opportunities unfolding may therefore induce diverse pressures on the business.

The business would understand that in order to address the opportunity internal changes necessitated like strengthening the organizational team to cover technology, innovation, building new processes, upgrade business practices and so on which in turn is needed to help the business to produce the envisaged positive growth, revenue and profit outcomes.

# CHAPTER FOUR

# KEY ELEMENTS OF A BUSINESS

What are the key elements of a business? How do you know and understand your business?

The true description of a business arises from an accurate account of the elements of that business. It is also pertinent that the state of a business ,the intrinsic health and financial worth and wellness of that business is best assessed and holistically understood by examining the basic parts or facets of the business which in totality reflect the complete picture of the organization in all its detail.

In order to understand the elements of a business in the context of the particular business let us take the analogy of the 'Tree'. It is true that the 'tree with its parts' or its elements namely the roots, the stem, the branches, the leaves, the fruits the flowers and so on which come together in order to make the tree what it is, in other words, namely the tree.

Thus, the parts of the tree are mutually dependent on each other with their synergies and mutual interdependencies complimenting and drawing their strengths from each other and thus growing and surviving by performing their unique roles and functions to make the tree the single ever perpetual living entity.

This essence is true of organizations as well. The organization is what it is because of its various constituent parts which combine together and act together in cohesiveness, in harmony, and rhythm complementing and synergizing each other playing their respective roles and functions while always acting together to produce the envisaged outcome.

**Specific elements of a business enterprise**

Let us take a closer look and analyze the specific elements of a business enterprise. It is evident that there are several elements that make up a business organization, namely:

Ownership and the legal entity: A business organization has owners who hold legal and financial responsibility for the business. The owners may be individuals, a group of individuals, or a larger entity such as a corporation.

Management: A business organization has a management team that is responsible for the overall operation and direction of the business. The management team typically includes top-level executives such as the CEO, COO, and CFO, as well as middle managers and supervisors who oversee specific departments or functions.

Employees: A business organization has employees who carry out the day-to-day tasks and activities necessary to operate the business. Employees may be full-time, part-time, or contract workers, and they may work in a variety of roles and positions within the organization.

Products or services: A business organization offers products or services to its customers. These products or services may be tangible goods or intangible services, and they may be targeted at a specific market or audience.

Customers: A business organization has customers who purchase its products or services. Customers may be individuals, businesses, or other organizations, and they may be located locally, nationally, or globally.

Vendor partners and suppliers: A business organization may have partnerships or relationships with other businesses or organizations that provide goods, services, or support to the business. These partners and suppliers may include vendors, distributors, or other companies that play a role in the supply chain or operations of the business.

Lenders and Financial Institutions: A business organization may have availed loan and funding from Banks and Institutions or other type of lenders in order to financial its operational assets or working capital for carrying on its operations.

## Business evaluation

A business is evaluated by different people from different perspective for different reasons. For example the person evaluating the business could be an investor looking at the business to understand the potential for investing or they could be a bank looking to lend to the business or they could be a customer evaluating the business in order to enter in to a long term association or they could be vendor or supplier evaluating the business to decide whether to offer credit terms to the Business against material supply or it could be a potential person looking to decide on employment in the business concerned and so on. For the same reason, the perspective and the angle from which each of them will evaluate will depend on their individual purpose and their objective.

## All elements of a business are important

Intrinsically, no element of a business is less important as compared to any other element of the business. All the aspects are important and together contribute to the value a business. Yet it is important to understand that a perfect harmony and equilibrium between all the elements and their interrelationship with each other is paramount for the business. This alone can provide a sustainable and perpetual success outcome for the business.

## Equilibrium

In the same way the lack of equilibrium between the elements can also produce an imbalance in the business. Some of the basic imbalances between the elements, which appear minor and inconsequential , though not impacting in the short term can cause an aberration in the medium and long term period and thereby produce adversity, loss and failure. The correlation and establishing mutual inter relationships of certain sub-elements to certain other sub - elements can provide observable inferences and clarity and reflect in the overall assessment of business organization.

Number of products or product mix versus sales revenue achieved

Number of staff covered by Employee cost versus sales revenues achieved

Total value of assets deployed versus sales revenue achieved

Sales revenue achieved versus profitability achieved

Total value of assets deployed versus number of staff members and amount of the payroll

Business vision versus team size, total cost versus sales revenue achieved

Through correlation and comparison between the sub elements mismatches become self-evident and the assessment become clear and more accurate. Further evaluation and assessment of the business will be complete only with comparison of data from one period to the earlier period e.g.: one quarter to another quarter and data for one financial year as compared to the next year. If the person evaluating is the founder or the board of directors they can use the understanding to take counter steps to correct the aberration. In this way businesses become more adept at predicting the future and avoiding adverse and negative outcomes.

Many businesses which experience surplus cash liquidity position for a continuous period of time covering several past quarters suddenly faces a cash crisis all of a sudden in a subsequent quarter. It will become evident that the events that suddenly occurred during the first two months of the current 'adverse quarter' whether such event was caused by a management decision or unexpectedly certain investments eroded its value because of some untoward market induced factors lead to the sudden 'cash crisis situation' as compared to an earlier period of 'Cash Surplus'.

Similarly, adversity in the form of sudden mass attrition from certain businesses cause the business to report negative results in subsequent quarters after a period of financial surplus. Both the aforementioned adversities reflect on the financial and the business performance.

In the context of the above two examples during the Evaluation of the elements of the business an appraisal of the 'efficacy of the management and the team resources' in the light of the above two adversities faced by the business will reflect the quality of the management and their capacity to deal with financial management of the business and in the second example their capacity to handle the team in terms of devising people retention strategies and so on. Evaluation of the elements of the business in a holistic approach provide a reliable understanding and a basis for forecasting.

In other instances of businesses where for example upon death of the founder followed by a period of instability which may have been caused on account of the top management team transitioning, or the time taken for the succession or in another example where the unexpected exit of a senior director from the particular business suddenly causes the business to suffer loss and adversity in the subsequent or next quarters.

The point being made here is that all other things being favorable it is extremely important to carry a balanced evaluation of the management team of a business.

From the perspective of business evaluation though it is said that that mere reading of the balance sheet or the financials may not reflective of the 'full picture' of the business concerned. Yet the financial information available in the financial statements read with the other vital information provide quantified information with value terms. Financial statements become the basis to corroborate all the information about all the other business elements and to determine their true contribution to the value of a business.

Hence financial statements that are accurate and presented with all the transparency can become invaluable for the purpose of evaluation.

**In this manner we come up with the following observations :**

We could safely infer that a business can be considered to be well managed and healthy when all the elements are managed well and in perfect harmony and alignment with each other. Further the financial fundamentals reflected through the financial statements of the business entity with all relevant disclosures reflect and accurately evidence, to validate our understanding and inferences.

Understanding the elements, then understanding their intrinsic inter-relationship and inter-dependencies will be required for a balanced understanding of the business, hence correlation is paramount.

Even if one of the facet of a business is found to have a certain lacuna or a shortcoming, depending on the depth and assessment of the impact produced by such lacuna on the holistic wellness of the business, a realistic assessment of the status of the business can be determined.

Yet the purpose of the person engaged in the evaluation cannot be fully achieved if the evaluation is from the prism of the present and therefore limiting mostly because the assessment is merely expressed through the available recorded 'past data'.

Evidently, the objective will become well served when we try to understand the 'unfolding future' of that business that is emerging from its 'present', like giving a glimpse of what lies in store for the business. What lies in store for the business can be summarized in the form of future 'sales revenue', or 'future profitability' or the 'value of the intellectual property being ' created or the 'customer growth or new business growth rate likely to be achieved ' or the 'increase in market share vis a vis the past growth trajectory' that the business will scale and so on.

In the succeeding lines we will provide a brief and concise description of each of the key elements of the business for the purpose of introduction and for a preliminary understanding .In the subsequent chapters each of the above aspect will dealt be with in detail.

**Business Entity**

At the set up stage of every business the entrepreneur is required to choose an 'entity type or structure ' best suited for his business. This needs to be done after keeping in mind the details of the business proposed to be set up the type, nature, revenue scale of the business all of which need to align to the project cost, capital availability and so on.

In reality most Small and medium scale businesses start with financial limitations in terms of the founder's limited ability to bring in capital in to their venture .Even as a conscious prudent option the boot strapping process allows them to limit the initial investment on the setting up the business, which include the charges for creation of a legal entity for e.g.: incorporation of a company.

Some of them carry this principle while making a choice of the legal entity. In other words, the legal entity that is financially expedient and cost effective at that particular stage of the setting up of the business. Given that at the nascent stage of the business there is total lack of visibility in terms of the direction or the course of the business.

This may be true to the period when the founder entrepreneur is focusing on creating the product prototype or designing, selecting the technology direction, making contact with the Beta customer with the product prototype and so on.

Thus in the early formative phase or the seed phase many of the founder entrepreneurs may prefer a proprietary structure or a simple partnership firm structure for carrying on the business. Until proving their product market fit and validation of technology , acquiring their initial customers these entrepreneurs keep the option of evolving their proprietary business in to a private limited entity for a later date once they have greater clarity.

Yet, it is true that in the case of business venture that is principally envisaged to be a 'startup' pursuing 'innovative and disruptive technologies' aiming for an exponential business growth such businesses are more likely to have a need to seek external capital from Angel investors, Venture capital funds, Private equity funds as the case may be from their 'early Business set stage' itself. They are able to seek capital at an early stage on the strength and potential of the 'business idea', disruptive innovation, large enough market requirement and so on. Such businesses are more likely to be choose an 'incorporated entity structure' over a 'proprietary structure' for setting up the business.

In contrast, we may consider the example of an SMB business which was initially created as a proprietary organization upon the passage of time having grown the business to a critical size with a potential for further business growth.

At this growth stage, it becomes necessary for the SME business to evaluate whether the increase in sales and operations, the requirement to hire more senior resources, or enrolment of new vendors, acquiring corporate or institutional customers and so on would require a commensurate funds mobilization for funding the business growth plan.

And to meet the above objectives there is a necessity to convert the business from a 'proprietary Firm structure' to an 'incorporated private limited company' structure. Hence the principle that emerges is that as the SMB business grows and attains a growth threshold, there is need for an evaluation of the 'type of business entity' with a correlation to the 'stage of the business growth'.

To illustrate more clearly let us take the example of businesses that has attained a Sales Revenue scale and is therefore looking to grow to the next level by capitalizing accessible market opportunities. For that business, in order to achieve its growth objective, evidently, there are serious limitations while it is continuing in a proprietary structure.

For instance let us look at the example of an SME business which has identified the business opportunity for acquiring orders from a large institutional or corporate customer by participating in a tender based procurement process of that corporate concerned.

On account of their proprietary entity structure such businesses though technically capable in terms of team resources and infrastructure, even possessing the customer stipulated 'pre-qualification project experience' for taking up the envisaged order, the business is unable to leverage that business opportunity. The reason is that as per the stipulated vendor registration requirement of that corporate customer, even if a vendor meets the product, price and technical conditions, they will not permit vendor registration of a proprietary firm, in other words the vendor's business need to be an incorporated entity.

In this manner the subject business loses the 'particular business opportunity' to their 'less competent business competitors' only because the particular rival business has the requisite legal entity. In summary the subject proprietary business is completely disadvantaged from looking at all such business opportunities in spite of their technical capabilities and infrastructure availability and thus forces a growth limitation on itself because of the organization's entity structure.

Thus it becomes clear that there is a need to provide a 'state of balance' and 'equilibrium' between the 'legal entity structure' with the 'business scale achieved by such business till date' and correlated with its 'growth perspective' for the 'immediate future' .Yet the reality is that in normal parlance' even after understanding the imperativeness large number of founders entrepreneurs of SMB Businesses do not pay attention to the above rule while remaining indecisive for a long enough time on the need for a balance and equilibrium between their business and their legal entity structure .

While evaluating the legal entity as an element of evaluation when there is a clear equilibrium and match between the 'stage of the business' and the 'chosen legal entity structure' the business receives a favorable rating evaluation.

## Founders / Board of Directors

Profile of Founders constitution and background of Board of Directors also become paramount as businesses are judged by the quality, reputation, credibility, educational qualification, relevant experience of the top management.

Thus businesses which have a well constituted board of directors, and who follow sound corporate Governance practices are accorded higher value by the stake holders, banks and lenders, and the perception created thereby help them in a large sense to even acquire business contracts from potential customers or raise equity or debt funds for the business.

In the case of businesses which have cofounders or co promoters, two or more partners who are well constituted as between themselves to cohesively manage the businesses, have the advantage of a sharing a common direction and ensure team work at the corporate and business team level. Businesses which are run by experienced professionals or a balanced and accomplished team receives a high rating. Businesses which have a multidisciplinary founder team or board or top management team which include technical persons, Sales person, finance and commercial person are considered ideal for the business.

Businesses are family oriented driven by family set up with proprietary culture receive a certainly different evaluation. On the contrary businesses which have a balanced board also consisting of professional directors who are nominee of institution or private equity funds maintain a high degree of transparency and disclosure of information and is thus highly rated They engage cofounder or shareholder agreements between the founder promoter and other shareholders which reinforces the bond and commitment towards stable management in the best interest of the stake holders and the personnel who are committed to serve as team in the company. Such businesses have tremendous advantages when they have to raise finance through organized sources such as institutional entities, Angel Investor groups or private equity funds or venture funds etc.

The point that is being made here is that for the person evaluating the business a deep insight in to the nature of the management, profile of board of directors or the background of founders can be an invaluable piece of information while understanding the other elements of the business.

It is also observed that there is a clear relationship between the type of management and the type of strategy choices covering important business facets like sales, profitability, cash accrual or pricing or asset creation or debt raising or debt structuring or exit and so on.

**Company Staff / Managerial Team**

Another important sub element of a business is the workforce consisting of the managerial and the staff team.

It is also relevant to note that Businesses belong to different industry or business vertical and accordingly the role of employee team vary from business to business. At the core level intrinsically for all the businesses manpower team is paramount. However, there are businesses which is entirely people centric which are in general termed as service businesses such as a software services company, software product company, facility management services business. In the case of a manufacturing businesses there is a balance between the manufacturing assets and facilities and the staff required to manage the facility and the machines contained therein. So the evaluation of businesses in terms of the staff team will take in to account this particular distinction between businesses belonging to different sectors and comparison with peer businesses.

Comparison with the peer businesses in the same industry provide invaluable insights in to the larger factors many of which are external and industry wide. They in turn induce internal changes and cause new pain points to occur in that business sector. This evaluation provides early warning signals for the business and to prepare the business to deal with the growing problem while it is still in the nascent stage.

In the evaluation of the managerial team and the staff team within a business, number of factors contribute value to the evaluation which may be as follows:

A business with a clearly defined HR strategy covering talent acquisition is likely to have a greater number of productive staff as compared to another peer business.

A business with a clear HR strategy covering people retention is likely to suffer substantially lower manpower attrition challenges as compared with the peer business and the industry average.

A business with sound HR processes that are effectively implemented is likely to have higher team productivity besides people retention lower attrition and work-related interventions.

A business with a better work culture is likely to fair much better than their peer competitor in the medium and long term.

As a summary we may infer the following: Businesses are valued by the quality and competence of the staff team and resources. In a well constituted business which has a balanced organizational team across the different departments and team members possessing the requisite skill sets matching with their roles, are more likely to have extremely congenial working atmosphere and employee culture. Such businesses normally have low attrition rates with large number of their team members being part of the business for long intervals many of them being part of the business since its inception. These businesses are more likely to evaluated more favorably and with potential investors agreeing for higher business valuations.

The discussion about the products or solution or service dealt with by the business raise the important questions namely:

Is the product designed and manufactured by the business?

Or is the product traded by the business

The same question will apply to the case of solution or the services.

A business which has its own technology, design, or knowledge, all or any of them which it uses in order to manufacture the product will therefore belong to one specific category.

A business which does not own the technology instead deals with the same in the form of a trader or a system integrator partner or servicing partner comes in a different category.

The way the business is understood and evaluated will depend on this major distinction.

If the business is depending on its own technology the assessment and evaluation will focus on the value of the technology the longevity novelty innovation differentiation and such other factor will reflect the value of the product under evaluation.

If the business is depending on the technology product or solution of another party or business or brand the existence of the business is heavily leveraged on the life and continuity of such business relationship. The evaluation of the relationship with such a party will become one of the value determinant of such a business entity. If the brand concerned is a reputed with many years of standing it will render a certain higher value and vice versa.

If the business is however dealing in products and solutions that is created by itself the discussion can proceed forward and examine many other questions

The evaluation of a business commence from the products, the product mix or the product segments or the product range. The diversity, the corresponding markets and business verticals they pertain to.

From the evaluation perspective the discussion about product solutions services will be incomplete without an evaluation of how the business engage with the market and through the market place reach the end customer this is termed and understood by most people as Business model.

It is not in doubt that business model is as important as the product dealt with by the business. Sound and perfect business model can make a business to be what it is and a wrong business model can cause a perfect product or solution to fail.

Irrespective of the merit of the product or solution businesses have to painstakingly go through the process of identifying the right business model fit that is most suited for the business. In the process of exploring they go wrong and even recur cash losses. But once they have discovered the model that works best for the business, the business can rely and adhere to the model to make it produce the desired outcome while providing growth and stability.

Business model can be said to be 'direct' or may be described as 'Direct Sales 'where the business which being the brand owner is in direct engagement with the end customer.

In the same way ,business model where the business engages with the end customer indirectly through a channel or another intermediary business and which intermediary being called a dealer or a distributor or a channel partner is described as 'channel sales'.

Now when the said business is selling the product through an online portal it is called 'Online Sales'.

Irrespective of the model they choose, a business is evaluated by the strength of their sales engagement with the customer by engaging different approaches whether direct or indirect in order to reach the end customer.

The sales Approaches that a business resort to address different opportunities and gain market access for their products or solutions and thereby reach customers across wide geographies without their own physical presence for example that business which has dealer channels in multi geographies is able to access customers in different territories while minimizing the fixed cost.

Thus the value of the business will be therefore determined by the appropriateness of the channel and the sales revenue and profit outcomes being produced therefrom. Similarly, it needs to be borne in mind that the process of evaluation is incomplete without assessment and correlation of its data with direct identical peer businesses and their business model engaged by them. Mere similarity with highly successful peer businesses in terms of the similarity in the business model is not a necessity reason for attributing higher value.

Using innovation, businesses have created new and successful business model having understood the changing needs and aspiration of the customers and thus causing total disruption.

**Branding and IP**

Most Businesses pay great attention to establishing the brand identity for their products over the product life cycle of each of their products.

Branding and distinct product identity is paramount for a business which has multiple competitors fighting for the same 'customer's attention' in the particular geography.

Branding provides tremendous opportunity for creating customer recall and identification in the market. This enables the business to commercially exploit the brand to generate sales and create value through sale of its products The investment in the branding is normally amortized from the sales realization obtained by the business from the products sold under the particular brand.

## Business Valuation

In the valuation of a business, assessment of the intrinsic value of the brand is a very important component. The key aspect is in terms of creating and ensuring proper registration under the provisions of the relevant laws thereby secure the intellectual property (IP) and the rightful legal right over their use.

The evaluation of the particular business with the brands owned by such business will definitely cover critical aspects like detail of the number of years the brand is registered and in existence thereby actively present in the market .The underlying sales revenues both yearly and cumulatively generated by the products in turn sold under the particular brand from the inception of the brand concerned and an accurate financial account all of which reflect the value and the potential of the brand.

Intellectual property in various form held by the business is the other element which is paramount while evaluating the business through its constituent elements. There are many businesses which are technology focused engaged in tech development work as its ongoing activity thereby sustained through its in house research and development department.

Some other businesses pursue their product development and research objectives by engaging in third party research and carrying out the same through a research institution or a third party contract research organization. Such businesses painstakingly maintain proper SOP and processes , technology development road map and documentation to evidence the assumptions and the research basis and so on.

## Financial Highlights

The financial information regarding the past and the present financial highlights are primarily very important constituents to evaluate the financial worth of the business. This is ensured through the compliance and conformity to the well-defined statutory frameworks to be adhered for preparing, presentation and disclosure of the accounting information and financial statements. Past financial statements which are duly audited by the firm of auditors forms the principle aspects of evaluation.

Businesses are required to present a financial forecast or projected financial statements covering the future part of the current fiscal year in order to make the assessment of the business complete in itself.

In the foregoing, we have provided a brief summary of above aspects which are the key business elements just for a preliminary introduction to the subject. In the subsequent chapters each of the above aspect will dealt with in detail for the purpose of deeper understanding.

# CHAPTER FIVE

# PRODUCTS AND SOLUTIONS

**Product, Customer and Market**

There are three intrinsically connected aspects that determine the success and wellbeing of a business. They are Product ,Customer and the Market .We will commence the discussion with the first subject namely the 'Product or Solution'.

**Product, Solution, Service**

The Perfect product or solution

Let us kick start the discussion by understanding certain fundamental aspects regarding the subject namely the 'Product'. Every entrepreneur sets foot in the world of business by envisioning to create a perfect and appropriate product or solution that tries to perfectly and completely solve the problem faced by a customer. In the most ideal situation, the perfect product or solution is developed with the customers' problem in mind and completely aligns with the customers' requirements and expectations while providing value for money. In other words, the money being the price of such product or solution.

**Product Alignment to customer needs**

The phrase "alignment to the customers' requirement" may mean that from the customer standpoint, the product is manageable, easy to use, innovative, and possessing uniqueness besides being state of the art. Furthermore, the product is providing a distinct, better, and unique experience to the end customer. In the ideal condition, in the post-sales stage, the business is tracking the experience of the customer at the pre-sale transaction stage or while dealing with the sale transaction and at the post-sales stage, diligently tracking, and enabling the customer through a handholding model to engage the solution, thus serve and solve the customers' specific problem.

Over a period of time, as the solution perfectly addresses the customer's problem and provides the outcome to the customer, the needs of the customer also change and grow, and thus the customer will seek more additions and modifications in the product. New technologies, inventions, and availability of state of the art new hardware make it possible to functionally improve or upgrade the product and offer superior customer experience.

This phenomenon leads to the birth of new variants of the products that pack additional features while dropping past features that did not augur well with the customer and in this way, variants are created and offered to customers.

**Creation of the product basket or product mix**

In this way, businesses eventually create a basket or a group of products that may target a particular industry or a certain customer profile or different industries and so on.

Thus, within the product basket, there could be those which are classified as the principal products of the business and the other products which could be the 'other secondary product' dealt in by the business.

Through a process of value engineering, businesses continuously engage in product development exercise almost perpetually. In this way, the Bill of material will be stand modified and functionally the products become improved versions and will have the potential to become an independent product variant.

Through a vision to innovate, businesses create new product paradigms, new classes of products hitherto non-existent, and create a new aspiration in the mind of the customer even, these products are thus part of the 'new blue ocean' the other word for the new market that was thus created.

Well planned and perpetual new product development initiatives thus help businesses to continuously generate year on year new products and solutions and thus help the business to expand the market reach, adding new aspirational customers, and thereby improve market share.

## Product Differentiation through innovation

Continuous Innovation helps businesses to increase product differentiation and build new value propositions increase competitiveness to face the competition in the market. When businesses come from a higher technology sense while creating new products, they invariably succeed in creating more superior solutions that are functionally more aligned to the customers' new needs and changing aspirations.

Similarly, businesses may add certain products which could be strategic to its existence. Some of the products may be related and complimentary in nature and may be added to ensure that the customer has one stop solution and is able to get a complete bundle for their particular service application without having to go to multiple vendor sources.

Businesses may have their own products or in other words, those which are exclusively manufactured by them. They may also have traded products which are sourced from third-party manufacturers on white labelling basis and they may include these products as well in the product basket.

## Major transformation

Let us turn our attention to look at the major transformation in the current decade in terms of the way solution providers are providing products and services?

There have been several major transformations in the way solution providers are providing products and services in recent years the primary aspect being the paradigm shift to digital. Many solution providers are now offering digital products and services, such as software, cloud services, and online courses, in addition to traditional physical products.

This shift has been driven by the increasing use of technology and the internet in all aspects of business and daily life. The second transformation is in terms of the rise of subscription-based models. Similarly many solution providers are now offering products and services on a 'subscription basis', rather than as 'one-time purchases'. This allows customers to access products and services on a continuous basis, while it provides a predictable and stable revenue stream for solution providers. Yet another important aspect pertain to the emergence of 'as-a-service' models in other words solution providers are now offering 'products and services as a service', rather than as a one-time purchase. This means that customers pay for access to products and services on a pay-as-you-go basis, rather than buying them outright.

With the emergence of innovative technologies in the field of automation and artificial intelligence many solution providers are now using its potential with different end objectives such as to streamline their processes and improve efficiency or using AI to analyze data, automate tasks, or provide personalized recommendations to customers.

Lastly, with the increase in personalization and customization many solution providers are now offering personalized and customized products and services using the power of AI and machine learning and so on in order to meet the evolving needs and preferences of customers.

**Evolution of product and solution**

Let us take the example of the following unicorns to understand the 'product and solution evolution' with regard to each of the brands.

At the inception, Businesses set out with a set of products and services and in the course of their life cycle they evolve, and their product gradually metamorphoses into other newer products based on innovative technologies with pathbreaking applications. In this way they managed to address change and the growing business opportunities arising from the changing customer perception , new customer preferences and a radical change even in the customer profiles. Let us now get to the specific businesses which are as follows:

Apple: Apple was founded in 1976 and initially focused on the development and sale of personal computers. The company later expanded into other areas, such as consumer electronics, software, and online services. Apple is now known for a wide range of products and services, including iPhones, iPads, Mac computers, Apple Watch, Apple Music, iCloud, and the App Store.

Microsoft: Microsoft was founded in 1975 and initially focused on the development of software for personal computers. The company later expanded into other areas, such as consumer electronics, online services, and cloud computing. Microsoft is now known for a wide range of products and services, including Windows operating systems, Microsoft Office, Xbox gaming consoles, LinkedIn, and Azure cloud computing services.

Amazon: Amazon was founded in 1994 as an online bookstore. The company later expanded into other areas, such as e-commerce, cloud computing, and digital media. Amazon is now known for a wide range of products and services, including Amazon.com, Amazon Prime, Amazon Web Services (AWS), Kindle e-readers, and Amazon Music.

Google: Google was founded in 1998 as a search engine. The company later expanded into other areas, such as advertising, cloud computing, and hardware. Google is now known for a wide range of products and services, including Google Search, Google Maps, Google AdWords, Google Cloud, and Google hardware products such as Pixel phones and Nest smart home devices.

Alibaba: Alibaba was founded in 1999 as an online marketplace for small businesses in China. The company later expanded into other areas, such as e-commerce, digital media, and cloud computing. Alibaba is now known for a wide range of products and services, including Alibaba.com, Taobao, Tmall, Alipay, and Alibaba Cloud.

In order to understand the product or services evolution and how

Businesses changed their products and services from their initial years to later part of their life cycle, let us take the example of 5 Unicorns founded in India

Flipkart: Flipkart was founded in 2007 as an online bookstore. The company later expanded into other areas, such as e-commerce and digital media. Flipkart is now known for a wide range of products and services, including Flipkart.com, Flipkart Plus, Flipkart Video, and Flipkart SmartBuy.

Ola: Ola was founded in 2010 as a ride-providing service. The company later expanded into other areas, such as food delivery, electric scooters, and public transportation. Ola is now known for a wide range of products and services, including Ola Cabs, Ola Auto, Ola Bike, and Ola Electric.

Paytm: Paytm was founded in 2010 as a mobile payments platform. The company later expanded into other areas, such as e-commerce, financial services, and digital media. Paytm is now known for a wide range of products and services, including Paytm Mall, Paytm Money, Paytm First Games, and Paytm Insider.

Swiggy: Swiggy was founded in 2014 as a food delivery service. The company later expanded into other areas, such as grocery delivery and restaurant management. Swiggy is now known for a wide range of products and services, including Swiggy Food, Swiggy Stores, Swiggy Go, and Swiggy Super.

Zomato: Zomato was founded in 2008 as a restaurant discovery and food delivery service. The company later expanded into other areas, such as cloud kitchen operations and online ordering. Zomato is now known for a wide range of products and services, including Zomato Order, Zomato Kitchen, Zomato Gold, and Zomato Pro.

# CHAPTER SIX

# THE CUSTOMER

**The Universe of the Customer**

Let us turn our attention from products to understanding the 'universe of the Customer'!

A business recognizes that in one sense its customer is the one 'who understands and articulates their latent problem and possessing a clear idea of the functions that the product they are looking for should ideally possess, the outcome that such product or solution need to ideally deliver.

The perfect product is the one capable of solving the customer problem while delivering great value, better experience better outcomes tangible and intangible medium and long term advantages to the customer. From a certain sense a customer qualifies as a 'perfect customer' when he possess willingness to pay fair value for the product or solution.

While creating products Successful business make it a paramount point to understand the strengths and weaknesses of the current product in terms of asking 'What problem is the customer facing with the current solution?' and seeking answers to the question as to how the weaknesses are functionally affecting the customer's business.

Who is the target customer?

It is true that the question of defining in very specific terms as to 'who is the target customer is one of the biggest challenges for most SMB businesses.

Before we dwell on the above question, let us understand the real implications in describing 'everyone as the customer' and whether it is serving the interest of the particular businesses?

One generation of SMB entrepreneurs who sold more general use products that had a large market with an ever-growing customer fraternity defined their target customer as the entire population. In reality, they were afraid to define the target customer largely because of inherent fear that the 'product brand' will be limited in terms of 'accessible' business opportunities.

These entrepreneurs were under the impression that it was easier to acquire customers when we define the entire customer population within the market as the 'potential customer' thereby without imposing any limitation caused by micro profiling.

Initially it may appear that this perspective rendered the job rather easy with virtually everybody appearing as a potential customer. In other words, just any potential user of the product was considered a 'potential target'.

This philosophy made businesses look at data and analysis of information rather dismissively and therefore they engaged no great effort, budget or technology to extract and analyze such vital customer data. They still did not get the idea as to 'where to start the sales activity ? because everyone was defined as customer ? so they faced the obvious question:

Should they start prospecting customers from the available contact sources within the proximate territory

In this way, they set out to tap the 'low hanging fruit' that was there to take next door in other words the users who they defined as their customer in terms of proximity the nearest the most accessible and easily serviceable from the point of physicality.

But to their utter despair they realized that these customers are not really the target customers whose requirement correctly and appropriately align with the features of the solution and thereby not likely to create great value for the end customer. This affects the way in which such customer views the product or solution.

In essence, they learnt the hard truth that there is no short road to identifying the ideal customer. early enough many Businesses understood that their journey to reach the destination called the 'ideal customer' cannot be ever given up until that destination is reached.

It is pertinent that it may take some businesses a few years even to such a customer but given their perseverance tenacity and determination they ultimately reach that point. This may take the business to travel beyond its home territory to new geographies, new terrains and even new business world in another country. Once they have proved their product or solution at the ideal customer's end where that be , the product brand realizes the true value of its products or services for the first time ever in its entrepreneurial journey. There is no looking back.

Once the observant business has identified the characteristics of this customer population they may be able to devise strategies to go looking for more and more of them. They may understand and engage the right 'go to sales strategies' that will draw that particular customers class to their specific product or the brand. This opens the door for more and more similar businesses with identical profiles becoming customers and thereby promising scalability of sales revenue and higher profitability and the highest recognition and value creation for the brand.

**Who cannot be their customer, 'ever.'**

While doing so, it will be in the interest of the business to clearly distinguish 'who cannot be their customer 'ever.'

In this way, in the process of their growth evolution businesses and every brand player realize the big truth that in a large marketplace which has thousands of 'users' all those entities being users of services are not necessarily 'potential customers' for the particular business in question. In other words, all the customers requiring same or similar products are not alike when it comes to their buying behavior, brand preferences, the specific functional characteristics that they find greater value and besides which mode they prefer to buy and so on.

**When 'no one' is its customer**

In another perspective, a business which described everyone as its customer, thus failing to profile the customer through a closer analysis, actually led itself to a situation where 'no one' is its customer.

They face the reality that 'everyone' cannot be its customer though a large number of entities within the population may be potential users. In realty for many other reasons these so called target entities could not be their customer's given their solid very different brand preferences, specific technology interests , price /Budget imperatives and finally geographical issues that influence functional product outcomes and so on.

Chasing the prospective undefined customer target is as difficult 'as the task of searching for a needle in a haystack'. So evidently, to the question 'who is your customer' there has to be a specific and well thought off and analyzed answer, this is the classic and immutable truth.

Yet there is a customer segment besides being users of the product they fulfil all other traits and characteristics that make them an ideal customer for that particular product or services, and it is necessary for businesses to identify and distinguish them before it is too late.

**Target Customer Niche:**

In this way, we come to the discussion regarding'Target Customer Niches'. So every business need to understand their target customer niches within the market place. In terms of the 'customer profile' they need to understand which type of customers are more likely to buy from them and those 'customer profiles' who are 'less likely' to buy from them.

**Who is the most ideal customer'?**
So, the question that is now relevant is that how do businesses address the challenge of defining 'who is its most ideal customer'?

We have discussed in the foregoing that It is common for entrepreneurs to view everyone as potential customers for their business, particularly in the early stages when they may be hesitant to limit their target customer base. This can lead to a lack of focus and effort in collecting and analyzing customer data, and a lack of direction in sales efforts. Without a clear understanding of their ideal customer, businesses may focus on those who are easiest to reach and service, rather than those whose needs and preferences align with the features and value of the product or solution.

However, businesses that persevere in identifying and targeting their ideal customer will ultimately find greater success in terms of scalability, profitability, and recognition for their brand. By understanding the characteristics of their ideal customer population and devising strategies to attract more of them, businesses can focus their efforts on those who are most likely to value and benefit from their products or services. It is also important for businesses to recognize and avoid targeting customers who are unlikely to be interested in their products, to avoid wasted effort and resources.

**Ideal customer to Loyal customer account**

But in course of time the entrepreneurs understand that the business will be able to create sustainable value in terms of financially viable sales both from a profitability angle and cash flow standpoint only when the business reaches the real and ideal customer.

Thus, having identified such ideal customer the business provides product and services regularly to the particular customer a per the customer need. This lead to increased product and sales realization from business, more transaction with such a customer. When these ideal customers experience a certain degree of consistency in the products and services in terms of delivery, quality, price and so on, such customers continue to engage with such brand over longer period and thereby come to be called 'loyal customers'.

Businesses realizes the opportunity of converting a customer who used the services for 3 or more multiple times in to a long term 'Loyal customer'.Loyalty schemes are formulated for rewarding customers who make repetitive purchases , in order to engage with them and ensure that they stay with the brand 'long term'.This in turn helps the business to minimize the customer acquisition cost and increase the lifetime value of the client.

What is the advantage of creating key customer account classification?

In the process of sales growth evolution, Businesses acquire customers who continue with the product and the brand for longer period of time. Depending on the size of such customers and their requirement some of customers source substantial quantum of their requirement from the brand. And in this manner they become 'Key customers' who contribute a substantial or significant share of the business carried out by the particular brand.

Businesses then find it viable to create a process or service that meets the needs of the key customers and ensure that they consistently experience superior customer experience in every step of their engagement with the brand ,both at the 'pre sales stage' and at the 'delivery stage'.Some businesses even create a separate sub department within their sales force to exclusively service and handle the business with 'Key Customers'.

**Key initiatives employed by successful businesses**

For the sake of clarity let us summarize some of the key initiatives employed by successful businesses in engaging with the 'Key Customer Account' with the core objective of ensuring business growth and customer retention.

Customer segmentation and targeting: By dividing their potential customer base into smaller, more specific groups, businesses are able to better understand and meet the needs of each segment. This allows them to tailor their marketing efforts and create more effective and targeted messages.

Customer Survey , research and analysis: In order to identify and target their ideal customer, businesses gather and analyze data about their customers' preferences, behaviors, and pain points. This is done through market research, customer surveys, and other data-gathering methods.

Customer loyalty: Once a business has identified and successfully targeted its ideal customer, they work building long-term relationships and customer loyalty. This in turn leads to increased sales and customer retention, as well as positive word-of-mouth marketing and a strong reputation.

Customer service: Providing excellent customer service is crucial for retaining and building customer loyalty. This in turn include prompt response to customer inquiries and complaints, timely support and assistance, and going above and beyond to meet customer needs.

Customer feedback: Gathering and responding to customer feedback thereby help businesses to improve their products and services, as well as identify areas for improvement in the customer experience. This is carried out in a structured manner through customer surveys, focus groups, and other methods of gathering feedback.

As evident the strategy in identification of the ideal customers and the key customer account classification and so on produces a serious financial advantage for the business as it helps the business to Conserve Sales budget and even contribute to Capital saving.

Without a precise idea of the ideal customer, businesses are likely to burn their working capital and their sales budgets prematurely on the wrong customer leads and sales prospects without being ultimately able to produce sales outcomes. These businesses may not have enough money left for their 'sales budget' as and when they are able to finally identify their 'true and ideal customer'.

On the contrary, in the very first instance when the businesses are clear about the profile of its ideal customer, they are more likely to use the sales budget and the sales promotion budget more effectively to target and influence the precise customer audience.

The customer with the 'ideal customer profile' is more likely to see value in the product and they may be willing to pay the 'fair price' for the products or services. This is more likely to make the 'customer acquisition process' more productive and delivering more customers vis a vis the marketing and sales promotion efforts.

It is therefore advisable for businesses to achieve the 'product market fit' in terms of identifying the 'ideal and real customer' before going 'full throttle' with promotion strategy based 'money spending' action initiatives .That business performs the best which has prudently used its capital , by engaging technology and its resources to identify its ideal and target customer within a highly and densely ' populated red ocean market place full of many competitors and a wide variety of users and potential customers.

Why should businesses define who is not their customer?

Business which have understood the profile of the 'ideal customer' need to define 'bad customer'Similarly based on experience businesses need to define 'who is not their customer' and which customer segment cannot be a 'target customer'.In basic terms it may be said that the product or the solution offered by the business does not possess the attributes that appeal to the particular customer segment or in other words the range of functional properties or features offered are not adequate for the customer based on what such a customer is looking forward from the product or solution ,hence such customer cannot be a customer.

For the sake of clarity let us engage the subject by asking the next question 'what's is the importance of identifying and recognizing 'bad customer'?

Bad customer are those customers whose requirement may in fact match the specific product or solution being offered, but on the other hand the customer concerned is a 'bad pay master' with a record of abusing their 'vendors' through the process of inordinately delayed payment cycles and causing long outstanding dues or the customer concerned may not follow any structure or business ethics and so on. Chasing the wrong customer makes the business bleed on account of cash burn due to delayed recovery or non-recovery of sales consideration or marketing and sales costs and may be termed as a potential financial Risk.

Understanding the profile the 'bad customer' helps businesses to focus their attention, by ignoring certain customer profile at the outset instead galvanize their sales and marketing efforts as well as their budgets and resources to the appropriate target which offers a high degree of 'sales or customer conversion possibility ' and thereby help them to limit the customer acquisition cost at the envisaged budgeted level. It take a certain period of time before businesses are in a position to credibly conclude that for certain 'valid reasons' which is based on 'actual experience' a certain 'type of customer' or a 'certain business segment' are best avoided and classified as 'not their potential customer' or 'Bad Customer'.

Importance of having to identify the ideal customer sooner to avoid falling in the hands of the bad customer and depleting capital?

Solutions businesses frequently start by answering important questions such as: "What latent problem does the solution solve for the customer? What are the limitations of the solution? Which target customer will receive the most value? Is the solution perfectly aligned with the customer's needs? Which customers will not perceive any value from the solution? Is the solution based on disruptive technologies? Is the solution easy to implement from a customer perspective, with minimal intervention cost?"

Early on, innovative solutions may encounter customer segments whose requirements are not fully met by the offered solution, even if the solution addresses many of the major problems faced by the typical customer in the industrial segment. In this case, it becomes necessary for the business to map the solution against the customer's requirements and understand "how the solution is not aligning" with the needs of that particular customer, who is also a part of a certain customer segment within the industry. The business should then work on building a more inclusive solution that addresses the entire market.

It is important for the business to understand the value that the target customer receives while engaging with the particular solution. Similarly, the business should understand which customers are unlikely to perceive value from the solution and the realistic limitations of the product when evaluated against the typical pain points of the customer.

However, some businesses in the solution space may acquire a few customers in the initial period who appear to be huge business opportunities purely based on the size and scale of their problem and business. Ultimately, during the execution of the order, it may become apparent that their requirements are not typical and working with the client is like building the solution from the ground up again, considering the enormity of the modifications and new work required. Contracts like these can be the biggest adversity for the business and may be referred to as "bad customers." If the business accepts more orders from such customers, handling their accounts may lead to cash burn and the loss of valuable resources and may result in the business itself losing its business direction and purpose.

**Wrong Choice of Customer**

Let us briefly look at how wrong choice of customer can impact a business?

For small and medium-sized businesses (SMBs), one large customer can potentially have a significant impact on their plans and operations. While an initial partnership with a large customer may seem appealing and promising, there is a risk that the customer may have ulterior motives and use manipulation or coercion to achieve their own business goals. This can result in the SMB losing financial resources and even losing other customers over time. Additionally, some customers may only be interested in extracting unreasonable gain from the partnership and may abandon the business at a critical time, causing financial losses for the SMB. It is important for SMBs to carefully consider their customer choices and be aware of the potential risks and consequences of partnering with certain types of customers.

Importance of communication in reaching out to the ideal customer?

One of the important aspects of understanding the target market and the ideal customer is about understanding the importance of communication in terms of creating the structure of the content , object of the communication and the information that has to form part of the communication with the end customer .Armed with more visibility about the profile of the target customer the business organization may choose the 'best communication content and mode' that the highest likelihood of influencing the customer and supporting the 'customer acquisition initiatives'.

# CHAPTER SEVEN

# MARKETPLACE DYNAMICS

Let us turn our attention from customer to the market!!

Increasingly, many businesses who have products in the development process focus their attention on the weaknesses of the products currently available in the market and that becomes the principal end goal for development of the product or the solution.

Though it is true that this approach is likely to produce a competitiveness for that product which then can pay off in the form of higher sales revenues in the shortest medium term, yet it may not serve the ends of the business beyond that limited time window.

The real reason is that the competing peer Business is likely to work on identifying and addressing the real most latent problem that the particular customer is facing .They may evaluate on the competing products and identify the gap that all the currently available solutions have technologically and functionally .

Hence, while developing a new solution that align completely with the problem faced by the customer, they may have an inventive and original bend of mind while choosing disruptive technology to innovate on the core design and product architecture, with state-of-the-art components, alternate cost effective sub-assemblies as the case may be.

This may give the second business a distinct edge and cause the former business to lose the customer and even loose business opportunities from the related customer segment.

Secondly, in the digital technology revolution the possibilities for the connect between the product seller and their customer no longer remained limited to the traditional conventional approaches, where the direct sales resources or the dealers or channel partners come in contact with the customer and carry out the sale transaction.

Thus Brand owners and customers had an opportunity to come in direct contact with each other by leveraging the emerging online market place.

This produced a completely new business paradigm , that unfolded a new business opportunity that needed businesses to make a major internal transformation.

This requirement put enormous amount of pressure on many business players to upgrade and holistically overhaul their business in terms of better products, solution, efficient delivery, prompt after-sales service and robust internal processes and so on. In order to address the business opportunities provided by the online market place these businesses had to internally reinvent the Business holistically thereby moving to a 'total customer centric psychology' .

Similarly, businesses which relied on channel partners like dealers distributors and for their sales now engaged technologies to make these channel associations or product marketeers such as dealers and distributors more efficient more focused, more productive, and capable of delivering higher sales while maintaining lowest stocks , virtually zero receivable dues, efficient and innovative approaches to logistics and goods movement.

Innovative Technologies and possibilities for more connectivity with customers put more responsibility on brands to deal with customers complaints and after sales feedback instantaneously. Brands had to deal with after sales service issues with greater care and diligence. Subsequent sales and new customer acquisition in some sense became dependent on the rating and feedback from the old customer feedback.

Businesses had to increasingly work on their product quality and delivery to customer and work to the last mile in terms of determining even their logistics choices.

The new customer who is more well informed about the available product brands in the market with their respective merits and demerits thus became even more demanding with clear customer expectations with regard to terms like price, quality and aesthetics, besides packing and delivery.

Thus manufacturers and brands recognized the continuously changing buying preferences of the new age customer and realized the need to prepare their business to dynamically handle the customer expectation and turn in to a revenue opportunity and even a growth driver. Businesses realized the need for continuous upgradation of their products and services and the need for introduction of novel and different products and thus ensure higher customer retention.

As the customer world got more and more complex, diverse and unlimited, it became necessary to recognize different customer profiles and then categorize and group them to understand the behavior expressed by each client category. In this, businesses understood the need for specific approach in its marketing promotional initiatives when it dealt with one specific class of customer.

Having thus profiled and tracked the customer class and identified their product preferences business understood the behavioral preferences in terms of whether they were more comfortable buying online or whether they preferred and trusted the traditional offline approach directly interacting with the sales personnel or through the channel partner consisting of dealers and distributor. Within the online preference while many customer preferred the online portals like amazon other also preferred the company's business e commerce portal.

**Product Market Fit**

In the early formative phase it is important for businesses to painstakingly survey and size the market, focus their attention and resources more accurately to attain the precise 'product - customer- market fit'.Businesses need to reach this point as soon as it can with minimum budget and in shortest time frames.

Once businesses achieve the 'Product market fit' businesses then become more knowledgeable to understand 'who else can be customer', more like the ideal customer and accordingly they can apply the capital to the right sales strategy focused on the ideal customer. We will discuss 'product market fit 'in greater detail in the subsequent paragraphs.

What is the meaning of product market share?

Product market share refers to the percentage of sales or revenue that a product or brand generates within a particular market. It is a measure of the popularity and market presence of a product or brand relative to its competitors.

Product market share can be an important metric for businesses to track, as it can provide insight into the relative success of a product or brand in the market. A high market share can indicate strong demand for a product or brand and can also provide leverage in negotiations with suppliers and distributors.

Let us look at the typical approaches adopted by businesses and brands to increase market share?

It needs to be understood that increasing product market share can be an important goal for businesses looking to gain a competitive advantage in the market. Some of the ways that businesses can engage to increase their product market share, may include the following namely Improving the quality and features of their products or services. Secondly Developing effective marketing and advertising campaigns to increase brand awareness and demand. Expanding distribution channels to make the product or service more widely available can be the another approach. As another approach Businesses can attract more customers by Offering competitive pricing for its products and delivering better value for money. Business can engage and develop strategic partnerships or strategic alliances to increase the reach and visibility of the product or brand.

We may now examine an important question that faces every business namely: what is the importance of defining and understanding the market?

At the core, businesses had to understand the market place. In other words it becomes necessary for businesses to study and survey the market place more deeply address many questions like : is the business in red ocean ?A term that means the business is surrounded by 'competitors' in other words a 'highly competitive market place'.next question would be : which is the market segment within that identified market place that are being specifically targeted? Who is the customer for the services? Who is not the ideal customer? and so on.

The next connected question would be what is the importance of understanding competition?

It became necessary for businesses to understand their 'Peer business who have identical product or solution offerings, 'in other words identifying potentially competing players who were offering similar products - almost a hundred percent identical - who are businesses which are direct competition etc. Similarly, with a more focused study and setting some specific criteria identifying the top 2 competitors was necessary? Similarly, identifying all the other competitors present in the same market and competing not entirely with wholly identical products, and also determining whether there are other emerging and potential competitors in the making and so on.

Competitiveness of the product brand vis a vis their Peer competitors became important area of concern in order to protect and grow the market share. The precise positioning and the market share of each brand vis a vis the other was an important aspect that determined the value of the brand and the growth potential that was available.

Before considering specific aspects like product differentiation and value proposition let us understand the meaning of a popular description of the market with the question namely:

## The Red Ocean market

What is meant by red ocean market? from business perspective? what are the business strategies to compete in red ocean market?

A red ocean market refers to a highly competitive market in which there are many established players, and the market is saturated. In a red ocean market, companies compete against each other for a share of the existing market demand. The term "red ocean" is used to describe this market because the market is depicted as a metaphorical "ocean" that is "red" with the blood of the companies that are competing in such a marketplace.

A "red ocean" market is one that is highly competitive and saturated, with existing players vying for market share. In a red ocean market, businesses may find it difficult to differentiate themselves and may need to rely on price competition and other tactics in order to attract customers. The idea of a red ocean market is contrasted with a "blue ocean" market, which represents a market or industry that is not yet competitive or fully exploited by businesses, offering an opportunity for businesses to create and capture new demand.

The concept of a red ocean market is often associated with the idea of a "zero-sum game," in which one business's gain is another's loss. In a red ocean market, businesses may be more focused on defending their existing market share and competing with each other, rather than on creating new value and capturing new demand. As a result, the competition in a red ocean market can be intense, and businesses may need to continuously adapt and evolve their strategies to stay competitive.

Depending on the type of industry and the product vertical Businesses engage various strategies for competing in a red ocean market may include Differentiation in other words Companies may differentiate their products or services from those of their competitors in order to stand out in the market by offering unique features or benefits, or positioning the product or service in a specific niche within the market.

Similarly, with the objective of achieving cost competitiveness by gaining

Cost leadership businesses may focus on continuously reducing their costs through value engineering and innovation and thus become capable in offering lower prices than their competitors. This may also involve other initiatives like streamlining operations, reducing waste, and finding more efficient operation models and so on.

Customer focus is another core aspect by which brands ensure excellence in customer service and building strong relationships with their customers in order to differentiate themselves from their competitors in the red ocean market scenario and build loyalty.

Businesses in the red ocean market consciously engage Innovation through structured R&D (Research and development) to grow and thereby continuously introduce new products or services that meet the evolving and changing needs of their customers.

What is the meaning of blue ocean in business context?

In business, the concept of a "blue ocean" refers to a market or industry that is not yet competitive, or one that has not yet been fully exploited by businesses. This can provide an opportunity for businesses to create and capture new demand, rather than competing in a crowded and saturated market. The idea of a blue ocean is contrasted with a "red ocean," which represents a market or industry that is already highly competitive and saturated.

The concept of a blue ocean was first introduced in the book "Blue Ocean Strategy," which advocates for businesses to create and pursue untapped market opportunities in order to achieve differentiation and long-term success. This approach involves identifying and targeting areas of untapped demand, creating new value for customers, and pursuing strategies that are not based on competing with existing players in the market. By doing so, businesses can create and capture new demand, rather than fighting for a share of a limited market.

What is the meaning of red ocean market?

It now becomes relevant to analyze the meaning of two terms namely product differentiation and product value proposition which have been used in our discussions Hence let us start by analyzing the question namely:

## Product differentiation

What is the meaning of product differentiation?

Product differentiation refers to the process of creating a unique and distinct product that is different from comparable products offered by competitors. The goal of product differentiation is to make a product stand out in the market and to differentiate it from similar products, so that it is perceived as being more valuable or desirable to consumers.

There are many ways that companies can differentiate their products, including through the use of unique features, design, branding, packaging, or quality. For example, a company that sells smartphones might differentiate its product by offering a larger screen, longer battery life, or more advanced camera than its competitors.

Product differentiation is an important strategy for businesses, as it can help them to attract and retain customers, increase their market share, and differentiate themselves from their competitors. By differentiating their products, businesses can create a unique value proposition for their customers and build brand loyalty.

However, it's important for businesses to be careful when implementing product differentiation strategies, as it can be costly and time-consuming to develop and market unique products. It's also important for businesses to continuously monitor and assess the effectiveness of their product differentiation efforts in order to ensure that they are delivering value to their customers and contributing to the overall success of the business.

The next subject that call for clarity is the question namely :

## Value proposition

What is the meaning of value proposition?

A value proposition is a statement that clearly and concisely communicates the benefits and value that a product or service offers to its customers. It is a key element of a company's marketing and sales efforts, as it helps to differentiate the company's products or services from those of its competitors and convince potential customers to choose the company's offerings over others.

It is thus not in doubt that an effective value proposition can be a powerful tool for businesses, as it can help to attract and retain customers, increase sales, and differentiate the company's products or services in the market.

A value proposition should be focused on the customer and should clearly communicate how the company's product or service will meet the customer's needs and solve their problems. It should be based on a thorough understanding of the customer's needs, preferences, and pain points, and should be tailored to the specific audience being targeted. The key components that should be included in a value proposition:

Unique value: The value proposition should highlight the unique features or benefits of the product or service that set it apart from competitors.

Customer benefits: The value proposition should clearly communicate the benefits that the product or service will provide to the customer.

Proof: The value proposition should provide evidence or examples to support the claims made about the product or service.

Target market: The value proposition should specify the target market or audience that the product or service is intended for.

Our discussions about Red Ocean market makes the following question relevant:

What is the relevance of Product positioning?

It was necessary for businesses to factually assess as to 'where the particular business stood in terms of positioning vis a vis competition?'Questions such as 'whether the business is in the 'Me too segment' or is the business predominantly in the 'Me better segment' ?

Businesses which operated in the red sea market scenario operated alongside number of competitors in 'breakneck' like tough situation struggling to stay and survive and fearing the threat of extinction and displacement through the process called 'Law of substitution'

Yet, many of these businesses fought hard putting all their financial and financial resources at stake. Those businesses with true aspiration decided not to give up and instead through the realization that they have to innovate and create differentiating products engaged in innovation and product development in the best manner possible to them. This they improved their products vis a vis their peer competing businesses. They could offer new and different features, through the use of latest hardware they offered more robust user friendly products and even functionally better solutions to the customer as compared to their peer competitors. In this way they stood distinct and were clearly 'Me Better'.They could retain their market share and their customer loyalty and aspire for increasing their market footprint. They could safeguard their profitability while being able to deal with flexibility in pricing and so on.

These businesses invented the concept of creating the ' customer ecosystem ' which made it possible for businesses to create a web of interdependent products that communicated and complimented each other delivering great value to the customer through their co-existence and thus helped the business to cross sell and upsell and expand the sales footprint through its existing customer besides adding new customers to the build their customer family fraternity.

The last few decades saw businesses which took innovation as the core business ethos and built innovative products and technologies that ultimately caused market disruption and manifested to even create a new market space a 'blue Ocean' hitherto nonexistent and thus catapulted the growth and the sales revenues of these businesses to make them multibillion dollar businesses.

## Product positioning

Let us now summarize our understanding of the product positioning with a structured summary that sums up the meaning of product positioning?

Product positioning refers to the way in which a product or service is presented to and perceived by customers in the market. It involves positioning the product or service in the minds of customers in a way that differentiates it from competitors and communicates its unique value proposition.

Product positioning can be influenced by a number of factors, including the product's features and benefits, its target market, the market segment it is competing in, and the overall market conditions. Effective product positioning can help a business to stand out in a crowded market and attract the attention of potential customers through effectively communicating the unique value of their products or services to potential customers and thereby increase their chances of success in the market. The typical strategies that are engaged by businesses are namely:

Price positioning: Positioning a product or service based on its price relative to competitors.

Quality positioning: Positioning a product or service based on its superior quality relative to competitors.

Feature positioning: Positioning a product or service based on a specific feature or benefit that sets it apart from competitors.

Customer positioning: Positioning a product or service based on the specific needs and preferences of a target customer group.

## Changing customer behavior

Thus discussing about customer and the market lead us to an important question which is what is the meaning of changing customer behavior ? how did the customers expectation change?

Changing customer behavior refers to the way that customers' attitudes, preferences, and habits change over time. This can be influenced by a variety of factors, such as changes in the market, economic conditions, technology, and societal trends.

One way that customers' expectations have changed in recent years is that they have become more digitally savvy and are increasingly using online channels to research and purchase products and services. This has led to an increase in e-commerce and a shift towards online marketing and customer engagement.

Customers' expectations have also changed in terms of the level of personalization and customization they expect. Many customers now expect companies to offer personalized experiences and products that are tailored to their individual needs and preferences.

Customers' expectations have also changed in terms of the level of convenience they expect. Many customers now expect companies to offer flexible and convenient options for purchasing, delivery, and returns.

In addition, customers' expectations around sustainability and corporate responsibility have increased. Many customers now expect companies to be environmentally and socially responsible, and they may be more likely to purchase from companies that align with their values.

Understanding and anticipating changing customer behavior is important for businesses to stay competitive and meet the evolving needs and preferences of their customers. It's important for businesses to regularly assess and adapt to changes in customer behavior in order to maintain and grow their customer base.

**Product market research**

Let us look at how businesses gather information and data about the market and analyze them in a structured manner to gather useful inferences which form the basis of their core decision making and devising strategies to achieve their Revenue goals. This process of gathering information as aforementioned is essentially called Product market Research. So let us now address the following question namely:

What are the elements of the product market research?

Product market research refers to the process of gathering and analyzing information about a product or service, the market it will be sold in, and the target customers being addressed. And thereby help in formulating the sales goals, marketing and Sales strategies evolve and validate the business model and so on:

The elements of product market research typically include:

Market analysis: This involves studying the overall market and industry in which the product or service will be sold. This includes analyzing market size, growth rate, competition, and trends.

Target market identification: Identifying the specific group of customers that the product or service is intended for. This involves understanding their needs, preferences, and buying habits.

Analysis of products features with Customers product features : Analyzing the features and benefits of the product or service, and understanding how it compares to competing products or services in the market.

Target Customer research: Gathering information about the target customers through methods such as primary and secondary surveys, focus groups, and interviews and interactions.

Competitor analysis: Studying the products or services offered by competitors, and understanding their strengths and weaknesses relative to the product or service being researched.

Distribution analysis: Analyzing of the channels through which the product or service will be sold, including online, retail stores , and other distribution channels.

Right order of things or order of actions

Let us dwell on another important discussion concerning products ,solutions, services ,customers and market. The Question is whether it is important for businesses to get the right order of things or order of actions to be performed? In other words which task or action item should be done first? which should be done last ?

More businesses and entrepreneurs have realized that getting the order of actions to be performed right makes the difference between a failed business and a successful business.

Entrepreneurs who have got the order wrong and backwards realized that in no time they have spent the money on the wrong heads ranging from untimely promo spends, mistimed administrative costs, wasted inventory and thereby being left with no money situation and now require to raise more funds.

The greatest challenge for the entrepreneur is to figure out why they failed ? and every seldom will they understand that this is the true cause of their failure

Let us examine the subject at a basic level. Ideally businesses ideate the solution around the most latent assessment of the problem that is defined in the problem statement. Market research, information gathering, data analysis, taking expert views and so on help the entrepreneur with more visibility about the market space that they are envisaging to enter through the product or solution.

This is a process of validation that provides a lot of insight on all the aspects not necessarily limited to perspective about the demand and the supply gap but insight about the most desired solution, the features and functionalities that are necessary, the attributes that are to be avoided, and the gaps and lacuna's in the existing prevalent product offerings in the market and the new features that would differentiate their solution both technologically and functionally from every other peer product now available in the market.

Thus, the solution technically and functionally evolves through its process of development and reach the stage of a prototype that is ready for a scrutiny by a customer who may be defined as the beta customer. through the interaction with the customer the product undergo further refinement and iterations and evolves in to a minimum viable product.

This minimum viability is endorsed by few other customers who may have also reviewed and revalidated the 'product under development' and thus approved the product fit for the commercial launch. The bill of material and the cost sheet and other detailing form the basis for arriving at the pricing while market factors the price dictated by other peer product brands existing in the same market also become relevant for suitable price fixation.

Given that price competitiveness is an important aspect. But anchoring on a price is a difficult task but an activity that evolves over time when the business meets with different customers and different product users thereby understanding the exact balance between the product features and the function and the parity with value and price expectation of the customer.

In the 'Go to market phase' businesses face the challenge of arriving at the Sales goal or sales revenue target fixation and determining the 'marketing ,promotion and sales expense' budget which is reasonable and capable of providing value for every penny spent '.

While making the plan businesses are likely to over spend on their sales and marketing initiatives. Businesses tend to announce product's which are in the development stage create an advertisement and promotion blitz which proves costly for them only to draw the customer to their doorsteps and then express regret for not being ready with the product.

In this way capital is indiscriminately burnt because the business did not simply get the order of things right. This is a prevalent problem particularly when the entrepreneur is able to access funds from their investors or shareholders without any restraint .In their early stint Businesses misjudge the quantity of inventory to be produced in the maiden batch and create excess quantities only to realize that the inventory may not sell anywhere in the near future, and may imminently become dead stock'.

The diligence required while determining the quantum of stock to be prepared or the quantum of promotion budget was absent. There was no realization that the business has very little information still very minimum data about the customer the sale forecast .So planning the trial production is to be taken up after taking in to various factors like availability of customers, their readiness to buy the goods, the type of products in the particular product mix that they are more likely to buy.

In this way, the business has to act with financial prudence when deciding the quantum of production and the financial investment that is involved in preparing the particular trial product batch.

In the absence of this validation exercise the business may burn their cash on creating an inventory batch which is larger than it can currently deal with in its formative period. When the business is in its nascent stage it is just discovering and understanding the solution and further its alignment to the customer as well as their problem statement, the state of the relevant market and the customer's real preference, their behavior at the point of buying, the factors which influence such behavior and so on. So the word of caution and the financial prudence and realistic approach can save the business in understanding the order of actions and apply resources in a prudent manner and thus retain from depleting its capital on wasted expenses and inventory

Before we close the discussion regarding products, markets and customers we need to address a question that is relevant for all businesses:

Why do businesses have to define what they will not do? what products they will not deal in? which markets they will avoid?

It becomes essential for businesses to analyze their past experience and resolve about what the business will do or in other words the products or services or the solutions that it will not engage in the course of the business. Similarly the business need to resolve regarding the markets and geographies that will be avoided by the business. In the same way by analyzing their past experience businesses resolve to stay away from customers operating in a certain industry segment or certain customer accounts itself. These definitions and stipulations are reviewed by businesses over the passage of time with dynamism and they may altered as when merited to do so.

# CHAPTER EIGHT

# RELEVANCE OF THE SALES PLAN

**Sales and Revenue Imperatives for Business**

The first thing that the entrepreneur understands while setting up a business is that he will have to sell. It is not in doubt that by and far sales is one of the most important facet and function of a business as it constitutes the principal life line of any business. Hence it is relevant to start the discussion by understanding how the word sales is commonly understood across SMB Businesses in General.

The word sales in general parlance in the world of SME is prima facie understood to be the Customer orders booked or orders obtained from customers which need to be fulfilled or executed .In this way when the figure of the actual sales achieved by their business in the earlier month is asked by a third person, entrepreneurs invariably report the figure of customer orders booked.

The Sales figures we are actually talking about is the Sales billing or the sales invoicing figures and not the actual order booking from customer. So, the word sales used in the business parlance is the outcome which is the Sales billing or sales invoicing figures. Invoicing therefore represents completion of all the activities from the stage of receipt of the customer's order till the product is delivered to the customers end in conformity with the customer's order and as per the terms contained therein.

Hence, sales from a holistic perspective is not merely booking of orders but essentially the actual sales billing done by the business or the actual value of sales invoices generated by the business during the relevant period. Hence sales invoicing encompasses all the outcomes of all activities up to the delivery of goods and generating the invoice thereon in the name of the customer.

Having highlighted the nomenclatures used in the sales discipline let us look at another perspective which would help SMB businesses . Sales per se need to be recognized as an independent professional domain with in-depth specialization in terms of skill requirement from the sales resources at every level within an organization business is as much successful as the depth of its focus on sales discipline. Sales is achieved by businesses by engaging a variety of different approaches and actions but primarily through a professional approach and following time tested best sales principles and practices around the sales domain.

## The relevance of the sales plan

In a basic sense, it may be said that a sales plan is a strategic document that outlines the actions and strategies that a business will use to achieve its sales goals. A sales plan typically covers a specific period of time, such as a quarter or a year, and it outlines the specific actions that the business will take to generate sales and achieve its revenue targets.

Hence, every business that is seeking to become successful should evolve a sales plan. The sales plan needs to completely align to the corporate Goals of the business. In other words the Sales discipline or the sales department become responsible to arrive at the sales goals for the organization and then need to create a perspective sales plan which comprehensively cover the entire roadmap from the goals to the sales strategies which help to answer the question of 'How do we achieve the Sales Target' along with the detailed action plans and so on and so forth.

Over the years, businesses attempt different business models to engage with end clients. Over time, the business model adopted by the organization also undergo changes and continuous transformation and improvements.

This takes in to account the changes taking place in the external world with changes in internal business environment. Businesses need to continuously balance both the need for 'survival and growth' and should keep in mind the need for business consolidation always following business growth.

How to formulate the Sales Goals for the SME business?

In the discussion about formulating sales goals it is paramount to note that the Sales goals need to be in sync with the business model engaged by the business and as and when changes are envisaged in the business model the correlation to the sales goals need to be taken in to account. Ideally in SMB Businesses, Sales goals need to be conceptualized at the inception of the financial year by the sales department after due consideration and validation of the following core information or aspects which are as follows:

(a)Past years Actual Sales data.

(b)Current year Business Outlook.

(c)Competitor Market Share Analysis and trends based on Survey.

(d)Sales Forecast based on Key Customer Client requirement analysis.

(e)Sales Forecast based on analysis of Sales trends pertaining to Channel Partners.

(f)Data on Regular Customer Accounts, Growth predictions.

(g) Market Growth opportunities, newer domestic geographies, international sales opportunities.

(h) New product development initiatives and proposed product launches during the year.

The above aspects are broadly the basis for formulation of the Sales Goals and creation of the detailed sales budget thereon. Besides the above aspects there could be many other specific aspects concerning the business for the year in question. These could also be financial consideration and monetary limitations or infrastructure or Capex limits .Similarly there could be other factors that concern the industry in general and which could impact the sales budget and the achievement of the same.

The Sales goal setting leads to creation of the detailed sales budget proposals. Ideally these are deliberated at the Founder and the board level in conjunction with the sales, operational and the Finance teams for the purpose of validation purpose and in order to arrive at an all-round consensus.

In other words, after going through the due process of Budget validation process which may cover meetings and interaction and participative thinking and brainstorming sessions founders with Sales department , operational and delivery department ,and the Finance department the budget proposal is adopted by the Board of the business which then become the Basis for the achievement of the goals for the entire business pertaining to the immediately forthcoming financial year. With the above discussion let us now understand:

What are the key components of a typical sales plan?

We have seen that by developing a comprehensive sales plan, businesses can set clear goals and objectives, identify the actions they need to take to achieve those goals, and allocate resources effectively to support their sales efforts. Some of the specific aspects covered in the sales plan are as follows:

The first aspect of the sales plan is essentially the Sales goals and objectives that the business seeks to achieve through its sales efforts. These may include goals and objectives covering Sales revenue, product market share, number of new customers, or other metrics. Secondly the target market in other words the specific group of customers that the business is targeting with its sales efforts. The target market may be defined based on demographics, geographic location, industry, or other characteristics.

The third aspect would be the Business Model in other words the manner in which the business engages with the end customer for selling its products or services. The next aspect being the sales strategies which is the overall approach that the business will take to achieve its sales goals and sales objectives. This may involve targeting specific customers or markets, developing new products or services, or implementing new sales techniques or processes.

The other aspect is with regard to the Sales tactics, action plans and key Sales processes .The sales tactics would cover specific actions that the business adopts in order to execute its sales strategy which may include sales promotion , developing marketing campaigns, appointing dealers and channel partners, or opening franchise networks or training sales teams. Implementing and upgrading existing sales processes, and sub processes is also a key aspect of the sales plan.

Further, Sales budget is monetary part in other words the fund budgeted for marketing expenses, sales team salaries, and other sales related costs associated with generating sales. Lastly Sales forecast: The sales forecast and sales Revenue projections depict the envisaged sales to be achieved for the plan period or the financial year and may be divided into quarters or months with subdivisions across product verticals or entire strategic business units within the Business.

What is the connect between sales plan and the financial plan?

The sales plan is an important part of the financial plan of a business, as it outlines the actions and strategies that the business will use to generate sales and achieve its revenue targets. The financial plan is a document that outlines the financial goals and objectives of a business and the strategies and actions that the business will take to achieve those goals. The sales forecast is an important part of the financial plan because it helps the business to plan for future growth, allocate resources appropriately and formulate financial strategies for growth and profitability.

By connecting the sales plan to the financial plan, businesses can ensure that their sales efforts are aligned with their overall financial goals and objectives, and they can track progress towards meeting those goals periodically through performance reviews and information and reporting processes. This can help businesses and its departments to make informed financial and business decisions covering allocation of resources, investment in new initiatives, and key strategic decisions to support their growth and profitability.

## Formulating Sales objectives

Business evolve their sales objectives as part of the goal setting and the sales planning which in turn clearly align with the business goals completely.

In order to understand objectives, let us look at the sales objectives set by a business which in the field of Water dispensing machines as part of the yearly business planning and budgeting exercise for their new financial year.

The particular business is already achieving sales from different sales verticals like 'Direct sales' and 'channels sales',besides 'online sales' . While focusing on acquiring new customers the business has put in place a process for retaining existing customers.

In accordance with business objectives set by the sales department of that particular business in the current financial year, the business is achieving sales from the following 5 sales avenue heads namely :

Sales through Existing and loyal customers* - 30% (sales/ AMC):

Sales through New customer/ new industry verticals- 30%:

Sales through New customers acquired through AMC- 10%:

Sales through New product- 20%:

Sales through new market penetration of the uncovered side of red ocean:10%

Sales from paying customers to be increased to 30 percent from the current 10 %

We have discussed the subject of 'Loyal customer' essentially being those customers who are essentially customers with the company for more number of years or at least a minimum of 2 to 3 years and 'paying customers' are those who do not avail the 'credit terms' and instead pay the 'sales proceeds' on cash terms and pay within the defined time period agreed with the client and incorporated under the head'Payment Terms'

Objectives help in channeling strategies and the action plans towards goal achievement in a balanced and holistic manner thus help the process of sales scalability besides providing the potential for an exponential growth in business.

When all five objectives as in the above example are pursued with diligence and passion the business is able to grow the sales rapidly as each of the aforementioned objectives collectively leverage the full potential of the business to address opportunities.

In order to set the back drop for the discussion regarding the imperative and the need for sales plans and strategies let us dwell on the critical question namely:

What is the reason many businesses fail because of 'inability to sell' even with strong products, technology and technical facilities?

There is no doubt that one of the biggest maladies and challenges faced by SMB businesses is their incapability or inability to obtain sufficient orders for goods and services or in other words to generate sufficient sales or identify sufficient customers.

SME entrepreneurs invariably tend to blame the circumstances and the external factors around their business as the primary cause. The reality is fewer SME businesses actually go out and really address opportunities in a strategic way either by innovating and inventing new ways or follow successful peer SME businesses to quickly ramp up sales through new sales strategies that can produce additional businesses, in terms of understanding, adopting and implementing newer sales approaches avenues and strategic approach to attain sales growth.

The biggest Lacuna in SME businesses is that if they are able to source sufficient orders through Direct sales avenue then they limit their businesses to that source of business. They do not have a growth mindset nor a Risk awareness mindset. For example if additionally they could access business growth opportunity by appointing channel partners they do not address the opportunity seriously....on the mindset that their direct sales business is currently performing well. So even though they address new opportunities for sales, invariably the efforts become passive and hardly result oriented. Further, they do not pay attention to the inherent risk to their businesses if one particular sales avenue suddenly drops or is extinguished.

In a fast changing market place where customer behavior is dynamically evolving and changing by the minute, businesses need to address different opportunity to engage with end customer by looking at different avenues, other words in more than one approach and thus ramp up fast enough to grow their sales manifold. In this way they will be able to manage the risk that can arise owing to dependance on one particular avenue...such as e.g. direct sales avenue, or as the case may be.

Thus it is clear that the paradox of not being able to sell is one of the biggest challenges that face businesses ,this may be a good place to start a more detailed discussion .

Businesses face the paradox for a variety of reasons which may include challenges with their business model, competition, and market conditions, lack of business planning and strategy approach ,hap hazard sales decision and team related challenges, this list could be still longer. And it is equally true that when the business in question is unable to effectively sell its products or services, it may struggle to generate revenue and may ultimately fail.

It may be relevant to quote the example of big Indian startup businesses who faced serious challenges in their sales and the ability to scale their sales revenues in spite of having raised funding. Thus for the case study purpose we may name startup businesses like Pepperfry an e commerce startup, Just Dial a local search startup, Grofers a grocery delivery startup, Flipkart an ecommerce startup and Ola a ride sharing startup and so on struggled with sales as it faced challenges with its business model and faced competition from their competitors all of which led to financial losses which impacted their survival and growth.

To initiate the discussion on the relevance of strategies we may examine certain fundamental concepts and realities that businesses face during their growth trajectory.

It is true to say that 'a business grows when there is growth in number of customers- not merely repeating sale orders from existing customers. And while the business emerges as the business leader the entrepreneur evolves a structure and business model which results in Exponential growth in customer numbers- period on period basis. And more specifically the business understands the function of 'adding new customers' is as important as the need for 'retention of existing customers'.

For achieving sales of their goods and services every business is continuously exploring new ways and different means to reach the ultimate client. Yet at the basic level, through a process of 'direct sales' in other words a 'B2C engagement' with the 'end customers, businesses manage to achieve sales. Businesses realize that getting new customers by throwing more and more marketing and sales budget sourced from its capital often creates a huge 'financial fatigue' in other words take them to a point of 'performance despair 'A feeling of hopelessness when the outcome is commensurate with the money and budget expended and that they don't have the capacity and can't do it anymore.

Thus the simple self-evident truth is proved time and again that the effort, resources and the time required in retaining old and existing customers could be a more achievable feat than acquiring new customers from the large universe that is called the market and the process may be financially less taxing. Of course, businesses have to continuously by adding new customers while retaining existing customers. To get the discussion rolling on the subject of sales strategies and the relevance for business let us look at some of the sales strategies engaged by successful businesses to grow their sales and meet their Sales Goals:

Common and Basic Sales strategies employed by successful Businesses

Lead generation is one of the primary strategies at the basic level. Structured Lead generation practices and processes involves identifying and targeting potential customers who are likely to be interested in a company's products or services. This can be done through a variety of methods, such as online advertising, email marketing, and content marketing, offline approaches.

The second aspect would be Relationship building namely forging strong relationships with customers to grow their sales by increasing customer loyalty and potential for repeat business and achieved through excellent customer service, ease of engaging with the business and customer feedback processes and so on.

Upselling and cross-selling is a strategy engaged by many businesses. Upselling involves encouraging customers to purchase higher-priced or more premium versions of a product or service, while cross-selling involves encouraging customers to purchase related or complementary products or services. Both the approaches help the business to increase its revenue footprint.

Price optimization and using pricing as tool to compete in the market and sustain sales growth even in situations where the business faces intense competition from customers is another aspect of Sales strategies . On one side, price optimization aims at involves setting prices in a way that maximizes revenue and profits for the business but at the same time the business does not lose sight of the need to deliver the best value to its customers and providing products at competitive prices. Businesses engage dynamic pricing, approaches in other words adjusting prices based on demand and other market trends.

Lastly Product differentiation is a strategy initiative which involves positioning a product or service as unique or superior to competitors' offerings in order to drive sales. This can be done through the use of unique features, benefits, or branding or any other means.

Businesses need to understand that intrinsically the real growth in sales revenues is actually exponential growth in the number of customers. It is also true that exponential growth perfectly validates the business model and the delivery model.

Through a strategy or strategic approach businesses evolve new way of communicating to the market, new way of reaching to customer, new way of delivering products and services, new way of engaging with the customer from order handling to billing, with the objectives of exponentially increasing customer footprint ,and achieving increase in product market share.

Businesses craft their innovation and product development initiatives by listening to the customer identifying the customers new pain points in the changing market scenario and understanding the nature of the solution and the outcomes desired by the customer and delivering that exact result.

Ideally, what does the customer really want? The brand needs to identify that. For example it could be the matter of delivery in 2 working days as compared to the current average which is 4 working days. It does not matter as to how impossible it may initially seem? Even if it requires continuous research and development to find a solution that improve the customer experience. if the whole organization works towards that objective with single minded purpose the business is more likely to move to the position of a brand leader and even experience an exponential growth in customer acquisition. We will discuss this subject when we take up the discussion of innovation as a key business strategy.


**New Sales strategies for changing business environment**

Let us turn our attention to look at how businesses have harnessed changes and developments in the external environment in devising their sales strategies and carving out different Sales avenues.

Particularly in the last two to three decades different brands and products across different industry verticals have demonstrated the power of creativity when it comes to devising different strategies to promote products and carving out sales avenues to grow sales exponentially. We have the example of businesses like Amul which have built huge brand value and customer attention to the brand through the theme-based marketing approach. We have seen businesses engage in negative marketing approaches in order to quickly build on public attention and therefore increase the sales conversion to achieve exponential sales.

Further in the last decade we have seen the digital transformation technologies and the disruption caused in every business sphere and the growth and influence of social media on marketing and sales initiatives of businesses and the ultimate sales outcomes. The technology revolution has opened up huge opportunities for businesses to acquire customer in more and more novel ways some being relatively cost effective through the social media.

Increasingly businesses are engaging social media through Blogging, Email campaigns, Placing ads in social media, Engaging influencers and all of which are essentially meant to aid the business to acquire customers and retain them. Traditional approaches such as Offline media advertisements, TV advertisement and other forms of outdoor publicity have been relegated to the side lines on a comparative scale at least for sizeable number of brands as the principal engine to drive sales opportunities.

Tapping sales through Direct sales, sales through dealers and Channel partners, setting up Franchisee network continued to offer scalability opportunity for large number of businesses. These businesses introduced technology and automation while engaging these sales avenues to increase the effectiveness of their processes internally as well as increasing the outcome from these channels or the partners in terms of more sales conversions more customers more business and higher volumes.

Businesses reinforced and complimented the pre-sales department by engaging vendor firms to handle lead generation and thus increased the customer leads or prospects and thus succeeded in increased in the volume of customer orders and thus increased their sales revenues. Business with infrastructure and operational abilities expanded their internal capacity utilization to absorb costs by strategic partnerships with other brand owners through while labelling contracts.

Many businesses managed to increase the geographical reach and continuously source new customers and strategic business associates by participation in trade fairs and exhibitions and thus increased their sales and their customer footprint across the country.

Through the foregoing we have seen that businesses invent and reinvent various ways and means to grow and expand their revenue, produce consistency in sales month after month by simultaneously engaging multiple facets for leveraging sales with customers all as a part of their Go to Market strategies.

# CHAPTER NINE

# Key Sales Avenues for SME Businesses

The sales avenue or avenues that a business ultimately choose will largely depend on a variety of factors, such as the nature of the products or services being sold, the target market, and the resources and capabilities of the business.

Businesses may use a combination of these sales avenues or other sales avenues that we may discuss in the succeeding lines in order to reach their target customers and achieve their sales goals.

Thus, the most commonly engaged typical sales avenues for businesses are as follows:

Direct sales: Direct sales involve selling products or services directly to customers, either online or Offline. This may include selling through a company's own website, a physical store or Branch Sales offices, or through direct mail or telemarketing and so on.

Channel sales: Channel sales involves selling products or services to other businesses or organizations who are retailers, dealers, distributors, or wholesalers who are engaged in trading or reselling to their own customers.

Licensing: Licensing is a process by which a business gives the rights to use a company's product brand, technology, or intellectual property to other businesses or organizations.

Franchising: Franchising is a process by which a brand owner who has a successful brand with a market share and business potential have demonstrated sales performance is intending to grow the business by appointing sales partners who are named as franchisees who carry on the business under the same brand name and using identical format and structure as defined by the Franchisor and thus produce huge business scalability for the brand.

Partnerships, Joint Ventures and collaborations: Partnerships and collaborations involve forming relationships with other businesses or organizations in order to engage in joint marketing and product sales thereby accessing new customers new markets and geographies .

Online and E-commerce: E-commerce involves selling products or services online through a company's own website or through online marketplaces such as Amazon.

While the above constitute some of the major sales avenues there are many sub sales avenues that are available for businesses which we will discuss in the succeeding lines.

The discussion on the sales Avenue may be initiated from the most basic conventional offline sales approach resorted to by business. In this way we may start by understanding:

What is the meaning of Direct Sales?

In reality there could be many connotations to the word Direct sales. One commonly understood meaning is that Direct sales is the sales achieved by a business through the sales team who directly engage with the end Customer. Businesses engage with end customers in many other different ways, one example being Sales through channels or in other words through the process of appointing dealers or distributors who deal with end customers.

However, a large number of traditional SMB businesses solely depend on the offline based direct sales as the avenue for generating sales. And over the period these businesses create processes to manage the sales function.

The team may comprise of Customer facing sales persons, Team Leads at supervisory level, Sales coordinators coordinating and managing the team activities and ensuring outcomes.

**Sales Growth through new product addition**

Let us understand the perspective of achieving Sales Growth by adding new products and Product wise Business Vertical creation that is engaged by some of the business enterprise.

In reality, large number of businesses achieve growth by addition of new products and thereby increase of product range periodically in a steady and well-focused manner. These businesses systematically increase their market share and footprint in the given market place.

For the purpose of better management and facilitating sales growth and scalability, many businesses create separate business divisions and sales departments by earmarking different product range for each business division based on some accepted criteria which could be either (a) products within a Common industry vertical (b) products that target similar customer profile, so on and so forth.

In short, the segregation in to separate divisions could be carried out based on the commonality of target clients, industry segment and so on. Divisionalisation certainly creates greater control and better performance by the divisional team concerned which they achieve through the process of installing sub goals. Some of them emerge as independent profit centers and may even called strategic business units or SBU's.

**Sales Growth through Creation of new Business Divisions within the Business**

In this manner, we have seen businesses creating different divisions depending on the nature of their business and their operational diversity.

For the purpose of illustration we are enumerating below typical business divisions in the manufacturing business environment.

Sales and Service Division

Manufacturing Division and Trading Division

Manufacturing and Turnkey projects Division

Division 1 for Product Category A and Division 2 for Product category B.

Let us examine the case of businesses who constitute their sales department in to separate product sub groups to ensure focus and higher sales outcomes. This approach provides specific advantages in a business which deals in high technology based product solutions that serve the needs of their end customers.

In such businesses, the sales department is reconstituted into separate teams who in turn handle the products and solutions and being assigned in the different product sales group, this results in better sales focus. This approach helps businesses who continuously add newer and newer products or solutions within the product range. Given the continuous technology changes across domains increasing technical complexities and greater customer expectations technology based businesses start experiencing the business challenges from customer demands and expectations.

It is true that new technology based business domains may necessitate induction of sales persons with relevant and domain specific skill sets. Many of these businesses find it expedient to divisionalise on the basis of the technology domains and the business creates these separate people teams in order to pursue sales opportunities with end customers.

**Key marketing strategies**

**Key marketing strategies for sales through B2B**

Some of the key marketing strategies for sales through b2b are as follows?

One of the most paramount strategy devise that B2B businesses engage is namely Lead Generation. Businesses formulate pre-sales processes that ensure identification and targeting potential customers and thereby make continuous lead generation and lead validation possible and thereby facilitate continuous increase in the flow of valid customer leads.

Well directed online advertising, email marketing, and content marketing immensely help in the lead generation process. In the new age businesses increasingly use networking which involves building relationships with other businesses or industry professionals through trade bodies and business networks in order to identify potential sales leads and generate new business opportunities.

Participation in trade shows can be an effective way for businesses to showcase their products or services to a larger potential audience and generate sales leads.

Businesses engage Content marketing involving the creation and transmission of valuable, relevant, and consistent content in order to attract and retain a clearly defined target audience. This is an effective way engaged by many successful businesses to establish thought leadership and generate sales leads in the B2B space.

Lastly, many successful businesses grow their B2B sales through the process of consciously building strong relationships with customers that nurture brand loyalty and repeat business.

Let us now understand the meaning of the term B2B2C?

Large number of businesses which have products which have a market relevance across the country have realized that the real way to growth is not be limited by direct sales with their home territory where the business is situated, instead they have taken steps very early in their business life cycle to create a scalability strategy by appointing dealers and distributors or stockists retailers and so on in territories where the business and the products have potential.

Through the appointment and creation of dealer chains in different geographies within the country to reach the target customers, these businesses succeeded in steadily creating a sales revenue growth path in terms of enrolling more and more dealer organizations, sales teams or people to indirectly work for the product sales promotion.

So in summary, B2B2C, or business-to-business-to-consumer, refers to a type of business model in which a company sells its products or services to other businesses, which then sell those products or services to consumers. In a B2B2C model, the company operates as a supplier to other businesses, which act as intermediaries between the company and the end consumers.

For example, a manufacturer of consumer electronics may sell its products to retailers, who then sell those products to consumers. In this case, the manufacturer operates in a B2B2C model, as it sells its products to other businesses (the retailers) which then sell those products to consumers.

B2B2C models have immensely benefited businesses both big and small particularly in larger businesses where there are complex supply chains and multiple intermediaries involved in the distribution of products or services. They can be an effective way for companies to reach end consumers without having to deal directly with them, and can help companies focus on their core competencies while relying on other channel partner businesses to handle distribution and marketing.

Over a period of time, these businesses perfected their dealer appointment and management policies and their internal processes for optimizing the dealer appointment and management system as a whole. In this way systematically the businesses built a strong network of loyal dealers which eventually became a strong business and financial backbone for the company.

Over a period of time, every industry segment has built their own practices around the channel partner arrangements and thus there is a diversity in terms of the dealer systems and the various tiers within the dealer distributor chain depending on the type of industry .For example in the FMCG sector the hierarchy within the channels network includes the following constituents namely: Dealers, Distributors, Super Stockists, C & F Agents and so on.

**Key marketing strategies for sales through B2B2C**

Let us now understand the key strategies that businesses adopt in order to increase sales through B2B2C or through the dealers, channel partner network.

It is Businesses that are heavily dependent on B2B2C continuously devise newer and newer strategies to increase sales traction through their channel partners or dealers.

Developing a clear marketing strategy in conjunction with the channel partners help businesses to be able to target niche customer segments with high probability for sales conversion besides growth and business scalability.

Offering high-quality products or services is essential for driving sales through the channel partnership. Continuously working on new product releases with better functional capabilities help the channel to attract and retain customers.

Offering competitive pricing is paramount for the channel partners to be able to sell the products more effectively. The channel partner pricing strategy need to be dynamic and through constant Business review and interactions businesses ensure that the product are priced competitively.

Offering performance based incentives likes incentives, discounts, bonus, gifts and so on is a definitive way to increase sales traction through the channel partners.

Building trust and strong relationships with the channel partners becomes key to ensuring success of the channel arrangement .Structured reviews communication and exchange of customer feedback and concerns of the channel is extremely important to ensure higher business performance and long term channel partnership arrangement with dealers.

Business who rely on channels to sell their goods ensure that channel partners are provided with regular training on the products and solutions and provided with the necessary tools and resources, technical support besides marketing materials that are required to support the sales activity .

Examples of Businesses engaging B2B2C Model

For a deeper understanding of the B2B2C business model there are many leading Indian businesses and brands that have engaged this model as the engine of their business growth.

Overall, these companies use B2B2C business model to sell their products or services to intermediaries, who then sell those products or services to end consumers. This allows the companies to focus on their core competencies and leave the distribution and marketing of their products or services to the end customers through the channel network. We may draw the example of three businesses namely ,Tata Motors, Hindustan Unilever, Bajaj Auto .

Tata Motors, a leading Indian automotive manufacturer, uses a B2B2C business model to sell its vehicles to dealerships and other intermediaries, who then sell those vehicles to consumers. Similarly Hindustan Unilever, a leading Indian consumer goods company, uses a B2B2C business model to sell its products to retailers and other intermediaries, who then sell those products to its consumers. As the third example we may take the case of Bajaj Auto, a leading Indian motorcycle manufacturer, uses a B2B2C business model to sells its motorcycles to dealerships and other intermediaries, who then sell those motorcycles to consumers.

## Understanding D2C business model

Let us turn our attention to look at the direct sales models that are now termed as D2C business model.

D2C, or direct-to-consumer, refers to a type of business model in which a company sells its products or services directly to consumers, without the use of intermediaries such as retailers or wholesalers. In a D2C model, the company has direct contact with the end consumer and is responsible for all aspects of the sales process, including marketing, distribution, and customer service.D2C models are often used by brands where there are opportunities for companies to bypass traditional distribution channels and reach customers directly. This can be an effective way for businesses to build relationships with customers by providing superior customer experience.

Examples of industries that commonly use D2C models include businesses in e-commerce, businesses providing subscription based services offerings. Some examples of brands that use D2C models include Amazon, Netflix, Dollar Shave Club, Flipkart, Myntra and so on.

In summary, these brands use D2C models to sell their products or services directly to consumers, bypassing traditional distribution channels such as retailers or wholesalers. This allows them to build relationships with their customers and directly manage the customer experience.

In general, businesses achieve scalability and sales growth by engaging different strategies and adopting different avenues for sales growth. We need to look at another business perspective using entry of the business in to new geographies as the scalability opportunity.

**Sales Growth through new geographies**

How do businesses achieve Sales Growth and scalability through the process of expanding their business to new geographies?

In their growth phase perceiving opportunities businesses establishing manufacturing facilities, for adding more and more products .But they need to achieve commensurate growth in sales and addition of customers and consistent sales month on month in order to sustain product volumes, capacity utilization and recovery of cost.

After struggling in one geography where there are multiple competitors businesses explore and ultimately identify new geographies which may be far away from the home territory but which is able to provide a sizeable growth opportunity that has a potential to grow volumes manifold.

So, businesses need to engage and put a strategy in place to continuously explore sales opportunities in newer geographical territories in a structured and focused manner to acquire new customers sustain growth in volumes, thus prevent downward sales trends,

When Sales growth by adding newer and newer geography is not engaged at the appropriate time it can affect the revenue growth of the business, and this in turn can even cause business failure.

## Sales Growth through addition of new products

Sales growth is achieved through addition of products, new product variants, intermediate products, bundling with allied products offering as bundled basket and so on?

Some businesses consciously work towards adding new products at regular intervals. Other businesses do not address this formally in a planned manner with predetermined time lines for product releases.

Most SMB businesses add new products as and when an opportunity for a new product is known to the business based on the information and feedback from the sales department with concurrence from the founder entrepreneurs. This exercise may be preceded by a market survey to validate the information prior to taking a formal decision to proceed with the development and launch of the product.

Successful SME businesses committed to their ambitious sales revenue goals which ranges from 2x to 5x or even higher necessarily formulate a Strategy to grow sales by addition of new products, new product variants, new product sub types which are technological similar or dissimilar or products which are different only externally in terms of aesthetics, but with functions remaining the same etc.

Consciously many businesses constitute a product development team being a core group within the organization handling innovation and product development activity

This core group who take up the responsibility to continuously engage by understanding the changing needs of the customer and engage in new product development which deliver better value to the end customer while meeting the customer needs more comprehensively.

Thus the product releases are made a perpetual activity with newer and newer products release once in a quarter as the case may be.

New product releases become an activity that aligns with the sales , operations, procurement ,inventory and finance department to ensure proper coordination and team work in the product development initiatives.

The product development initiatives thus become an integral part of the business scalability process and become very effective in contributing to higher market share through adding customers in different price segments and product choices.

Large number of businesses have achieved spectacular growth year on year basis by formulating the market Launch initiatives of new product or product variants in a process oriented manner as part of a consciously worked out strategy of growing sales and to create an exponential progression in the sales growth in a consistent manner. Let us look at another perspective namely:

**Sales Growth through Key Customer Account management**

Sales scalability through Creation of 'Key Customer Account Management' within the Sales department?

As businesses engage with customers who rely on the product or service offered to them and develop a dependance over time such customers become perpetual and loyal customers.

Invariably, the business is registered as a vendor with such customer businesses and slowly manages to obtain regular orders and sales from such customers. In some cases, the volume of goods and value of sales through these customers become sizeable and may constitute a substantial percentage of sales. Over the passage of time, these businesses mange to bring on board more number of such customers and manage to retain them.

These customers then come to be classified as 'Key Customer Account'.

Successful businesses slowly build a 'key customer Account' portfolio which in turn contribute a substantial value to the sales revenue basket on a month on month basis. Some businesses manage to book sales from their key customers which may contribute to more than 50 percent of their total sales. This in turn provides consistency in sale, regular product and business volumes and risk mitigation.

These businesses engage key customer account management processes to holistically ensure the management of the key customer account book which encompasses from the nurturing of a 'potential key customer relationship' and 'growing' such customer Account in a systematic manner on a period to period basis. No opportunity is missed ,for cross selling and up selling within the key customer Business. This is on the assumption that the designated key customer is a large business with different divisions. It is a possibility that some of these large customer accounts could even be pan country or pan world who may have divisions in other countries and international geographies which may offer scalable business opportunities.

Businesses which effectively manage multiple key customer accounts in a particular industry find that they have a good reputation in the relevant industry and such businesses become a preferred vendor in a particular industry and the chances of acquiring another customer in the same industry is relatively very high.

Key customer account management as strategy helps businesses to reduce the Cost of business acquisition. At the same time key customers understand their position and the dependance of their vendor to acquire their business set high customer expectation.

The expectation from key customer may be in terms of effective response at the pre sales stage and the post sales stage including after sales service phase. Businesses understand the imperative to appoint dedicated resource within the sales team who are required to manage these key customer accounts to meet their client service expectation from nurturing leads, soliciting orders , delivery stage to complaint handling requirements etc.'Customer obsession' invariably forms the central theme in the building of key customer relationships and effectively curtail if not prevent rival's and competitors from entering the key customers account.

How did SME Businesses leverage Sales growth through Online strategies?

Large number of businesses which existed within geographical silos unable to reach out to customers in different country geographies and even global location.

Inherently over the earlier decades businesses depended on offline direct sales approach. In the In case of SMB businesses the pre sales phase covering prospecting and validation of leads and so on remained a huge challenge required huge time money and effort.

In the digital era with the entry of online B2B portals businesses succeeded in obtaining valid leads which the business could convert in to customer order by employing internal sales processes backed by sales team.

In other words, through these Portals with a limited financial cost budget by listing their products businesses gained access to leads from potential customers who depended on these portals as their avenue for sourcing goods and services.

Thus, for these SME entrepreneurs such B2B portals became the pre sales engine and an important avenue for obtaining actionable leads which could be converted in to potential orders.

For the Businesses across sectors, these online avenues became a great game changer

With many of the businesses being able to source more sales leads with no territorial limitations and thus their business momentum itself increased .

SME businesses who moved to the online sales opportunities with B2B platforms realized that they had to completely realign and overhaul the entire internal processes to handle the qualified and prospects and valid leads now flowing in larger numbers from this source. This is in terms of being able to submit offers to prospective customers, in the shortest possible time and thereby improve the chances for conversion.

It was clear that typical customers sourcing products through the B2B portals having reduced their time for decision making and finalizing orders resulted in response time became extremely critical.

These SMB businesses needed to create standardized processes within the business in order to churn out more offers, quotation well in time without compromising on their accuracy. These businesses had to be fast enough with their correspondence and responses, submission of clarifications on their offers, well positioned with their readiness with technical presentations and product catalogues. Under these situations, standardization in pricing became critical factors for success. Many SMB players understood the sales potential offered by the new business avenues and reinvented their business internally to harness the opportunity.

With the advent of time more and more businesses which required to source goods or services moved to these Online B2B portals with the objectives of making their sourcing more expedient and cost effective and less cumbersome and least time consuming. The speed of making decisions within the procurement departments were more structured, standardized and faster and this benefited the entire business fraternity particularly the seller and the buyer.

In the succeeding chapter the whole gamut of doing business Online is elucidated in detail.

Sales growth through set up own e commerce website and direct sale online.

Large number of SMB businesses set up their portals with a e commerce dimension so that could continuously address the D2C sales opportunities with customers directly .

In this way, it provide a possibility where the seller Brand is directly engaged with the end customer effectively disinter-mediating the middle layer of channels, dealers and market makers and thereby establishing the ownership with regard to the customer account .

Some of these businesses went on to concurrently create retail stores either as a full-fledged store or merely as an experience center within the precincts of cities and towns to promote customer experience and effective sales conversion when the discerning customer needed a physical inspection or 'touch and feel' of the product before taking a decision to purchase the product.

A lot of emphasis went in to building the brand credibility, and customer engagement from the stage of lead nurturing to sales order closure. These businesses also ensured sufficient customer focus through after sales service, customer centric approaches and taking care to deal with reputation management aspects. Social media channels and digital marketing strategies became an important avenue to these businesses to attain more customers and sales growth.

**Marketing strategies to grow Online B2C Sales**

As a summary, let us look at the key marketing strategies employed by businesses to grow their Online b2c (business to consumer sales)? Some common strategies are:

Search engine optimization (SEO) involves optimizing a website and its content to make the brand more visible in search engine results pages for relevant keywords. This can help businesses to organically attract traffic to their website and increase sales.

The second strategy initiative would be Pay-per-click (PPC) advertising which essentially involve engaging in paid advertisements that appear in search engine results pages or on other websites and help businesses to drive customer to the website and facilitate sales growth.

Email marketing may be an effective strategy to reach a specific target audience and drive sales by sending targeted emails to a list of subscribers for promoting products or services. As an effective way to build brand awareness and driving sales businesses engage social media marketing involves using different social media platforms such as Facebook,

Instagram, and Twitter to promote products or services and engage with customers.

Lastly, Influencer marketing is engaged by many businesses to effectively reach a specific target audience and drive sales. This may essentially involve partnering with social media influencers or industry experts to promote products or services.

**Marketing strategies to grow business Online through B2B Portals**

Having understood the strategies for promoting B2c sales let us understand the approaches strategies to acquire business through online B2B portals like India mart or Ali baba.

Businesses need to Optimize and present an accurate and comprehensive business profile on the portal that clearly communicates the business's offerings and capabilities by using high-quality images and detailed product descriptions, as well as information about the products, the Business and the team.

Secondly, using targeted keywords in your product titles and descriptions to increase the visibility of your products to potential customers and thus leveraging the search functions in the B2B portals that allow buyers to find products or suppliers based on keywords.

Thirdly, Leverage reviews and rating features available in Online B2B portals that allow customers to provide feedback about your business and products as a practice Motivate satisfied customers to leave positive reviews, which in- turn help to build trust and credibility with potential customers.

Further utilizing the paid advertising options such as sponsored listings or banner ads provided by B2B portals in a prudent and focused manner subject to budgets will help to increase the brand and product visibility to potential customers.

Participation in trade shows and events hosted by many B2B portals will help to showcase the Brand and its products and services and offer a connect with potential customers. Businesses need to install robust customer response and feedback processes to ensure speedy redress to customer queries and Inquiries.

It is paramount to note that implementing the above strategies dynamically and aligning the same to the changing market trends , business opportunities help businesses to immensely increase their visibility and credibility on the online B2B portals and acquire new customers and grow their business through these B2B channels.

## Business strategies for scaling Business Revenues through Exports

Let us dwell on yet another avenue available to business for taking the products and services to global geographies through the process of exports.

One of the most important point that drives many businesses to explore potential export opportunities for its goods and services besides the opportunities to grow sales and profitability by accessing global market demand and customers is the fact that it mitigates risk factors in terms of the business becoming too dependent on the domestic market which may be heavily influenced by many factors that induce a seasonable nature of demand and lean period without any opportunity for sales revenues and possibility for non-recovery of fixed costs.

As a background to the above subject it may be noted that the growth of different economies across the world and the huge interconnectivity between regions of the world have seen a large growth in international trade in the last decades. Over the years governments of various countries across the world have laid emphasis to the need for the SME businesses to make foray into the export field and encash the unlimited potential that is available in international trade.

Governments have constituted export trade councils for assisting entrepreneurs who are looking to export in various ways including the organizing of trade delegations to countries across the world for exploring export sales opportunities in a more organized manner and conducting trade fairs with the cooperation of the trade commissioners from the fellow country and thus creating an organized platform for cooperation between the entrepreneurs in order to explore sales and purchase opportunities.

Historically, this has resulted in the creation of industrial communities within the precincts of metros, towns and the countryside and the villages which have evolved as a complete ecosystem for different export based products and components.

Large number of business have thus evolved as '100 percent export based units' focusing only on export sales while others have a risk mitigated model where they have a domestic sales division and an export sales division which independently look at the opportunities in the domestic and the export sales spheres respectively.

Around the international trade ecosystem a large number of global trading businesses which focus on buy and sell model specializing in certain products or a related range of products within a particular industry or a wide variety of products also emerged.

**Key Export sales Strategies**

Let us sum up our discussion on producing sales scalability through the process of targeting export opportunities with the question: what are the key strategies to increase export sales.

There are several strategies that companies can use to increase their export sales.

Firstly, Branding establishing a strong brand helps the business to stand out in international markets and increase sales.

Secondly, Market research is paramount to understand the needs and preferences of their target markets, which can helps the business to devise and plan the product offerings and the business Model.

Thirdly, developing partnerships with potential channels, Agents ,distributors, or other local partners help the business reach new customers in their target markets. Participating in trade shows help businesses to showcase their products to potential buyers from around the world.

Businesses engage with Online e commerce B2B portals to reach international customers for their products and services. By utilizing government export programs to expand product exports, including trade missions and delegations and ancillary services such as market research , export financing, export credit risk insurance businesses are able to scale up their export revenues.

Offering dynamic and competitive pricing for the products is extremely important in the export business field for acquiring overseas customers and expanding export sales footprint.

In the succeeding lines we discuss different avenues for achieving sales and when businesses pursue opportunities for increasing sales simultaneously through multiple sales avenues which are feasible considering the nature of the business as well as the industry vertical in which the business is operating and looking to scale revenues.

How to leverage Sales growth opportunity through formation of Joint venture with strategic partner?

Many Businesses perceive opportunities for revenue growth through tie up with their vendors or their customers or strategic constituents with in the industry.

These businesses who are looking to leverage business opportunities jointly in collaboration with the particular partner business enter in to a long term relationship by setting up a joint venture business entity. In this way they engage the group synergies to pursue business opportunities in a focused and mutually beneficial manner.

Perspective on Sales growth through private labelling or contract manufacturing for another brand.

Manufacturing businesses who have state of the art infrastructure and installed capacity to manufacture products are under stress to ensure sufficient sales volumes so that the manufacturing capacity can be optimally used and required amount of contribution is earned in order to pay expenses and meet financial obligations.

Larger Businesses possessing their brands which have large traction for their products across different geographies approach SMB businesses to process the products and label or brand the products in their name by entering in to a private white labelling contract.

In the private labelling contracts it is possible that the brand owner provides the raw material, packing material or any other input required in the manufacture to their vendor supplier. In other cases, the brand owner may not supply the inputs and the raw material and packing material procurement is the responsibility of the business processing the order.

Sales growth by becoming a Licensee of a well-known manufacturer Indian or international?

Businesses enter in to tie-up with larger players for assembly , manufacture, processing of the products as per the principal's specification which may be termed as job working contracts. This helps these businesses to utilize their installed capacity and thereby recover fixed costs through the job working or processing contract.

**Appointing trade representatives or business associates**

How SME businesses achieve Sales growth by appointing trade representative or business associates in different geographies?

Businesses looking to expand across different geographies face a serious constraint of having to open branch offices in the designated geography where they may want to expand and establish sales presence. These branch offices will require considerable amount of money to set up and recurring fixed cost on manpower, establishment and sales related expenses heads.

Instead of pursuing this approach, organizations identify experienced and very potential individuals who have past experience in the relevant field and good contacts and network in the designated geographies. These individuals are appointed as resident sales representatives or trade representatives on a retainer fee with reimbursement for actual business related expenditure. They are required to operate in the designated location and entrusted with the responsibility for prospecting sales opportunities. In this manner the business is not burdened with the recurring cost of setting up a branch and incur other establishment setting up cost like purchase of furniture, equipment and thus benefit from the asset light model.

**Appointing a lead generation agency for obtain quality customer leads**

Increasingly, businesses realize that they are not able to do everything all by themselves. In the matter of sales conventional business approach requires business to set up a team to handle the presages activity such as lead generation, qualifying the leads, engaging with the clients through a call as the prelude to the process of closing the order. On the other hand smart sales professional who understand the art of sales have created boutique sales consulting organization which provide lead generation services in terms of handling the entire process up to delivering actionable leads which are to be transformed in to customer orders. By engaging the services of lead generation agencies businesses can increase their market reach and acquire customers and potential business opportunities.

**Sales growth opportunity by appointing an MNC partner**

What is the Sales growth opportunity by appointing a MNC as your marketing partner?

Large number of businesses which have products which have outstanding value propositions and uniqueness with a scalable sales potential have been approached by MNC businesses offering to be their marketing and sales channel. These businesses have found value in entering in to a tie up with such big players which has the inherent potential to take the product across different geographies within the country and globally.

**Sales growth through large distribution channels**

Perspective on Sales growth through large distribution channels such as Defence canteen stores, special purpose cooperative societies?

The FMCG, domestic appliances and large number of industry verticals have created sales avenues by going through the vendor registration formalities of quasi-governmental channels like the defence canteen stores and other cooperative societies. These sources have large requirement and once registered there is opportunity for obtaining large orders covering substantial quantities for a longer period of time depending on the type of product.

# CHAPTER TEN

# Innovation and Disruption

**Innovative and Disruptive Strategy Approaches**

Having understood different sales avenues let us discuss certain marketing approaches and strategies emerging from these marketing approaches which have been engaged by number of successful businesses as the central core of their marketing strategy and produced huge exponentially in sales and customer acquisition leading to creation of brands which are market leaders in their respective field. Let us take up the discussion about theme-based marketing:

**Theme based marketing**

What is theme based marketing? how did Amul leverage theme based marketing approach to build brand?

Theme-based marketing is a marketing strategy in which a company develops marketing campaigns and activities around a specific theme or concept. The theme is usually related to the company's products or services and can be used to differentiate the company from its competitors.

Amul, a leading Indian dairy company, has effectively leveraged theme-based marketing to build its brand. Amul is known for its catchy, humorous, and thought-provoking advertisements, which often revolve around current events and social issues. To draw a recent example, Amul has used themes such as the COVID-19 pandemic, and in the past have used general political elections, and very often social issues to create memorable and impactful advertisements that resonated well with its target audience.

By using theme-based marketing, Amul has been able to differentiate itself from its competitors and build a strong brand identity that is recognized and trusted by consumers. The company's use of catchy slogans, humorous illustrations, thought-provoking themes to create impactful and memorable advertisements that resonated with consumers has immensely helped the brand to distinctly stand out in the crowded dairy market and build a huge loyal customer base over the years.

For the sake of recall and understanding about theme based marketing approach let us look at other Indian brands which have positioned their brands firmly in the market by engaging the theme based approach to differentiate themselves and build their brand identity through advertisements which resonated well with their customers and which contributed huge marketing mileage and business scalability.

Tata Tea, a leading Indian tea company, has used theme-based marketing to build its brand in terms of its "Jaago Re" campaign, launched in 2005, which used social awareness and civic responsibility theme to create impactful and memorable advertisements.

Similarly, Air India, the prominent Airliner from India, used theme-based marketing to promote its brand through "Fly the New Feeling" advertisement campaign, launched in 2015, using themes such as innovation, comfort, and safety.

Airtel, the leading Indian telecom player used theme-based marketing in the year 2006 for its campaign "Har Ek Friend Zaroori Hota Hai" Ad campaign, which used themes such as friendship and connectivity to create the brand presence.

Reliance Jio: Reliance Jio, another Indian telecom player used theme-based marketing in the year 2016 to build its brand through its "Jio, Welcome to the Digital Life" Ad campaign,, used themes such as digital transformation and connectivity which produced huge brand visibility and exponential growth in customers.

## The relevance of understanding 'Red Ocean'

We have discussed in detail the meaning of red ocean market in the earlier chapter. However, for the purpose of understanding sales strategies from the context of the 'red ocean market, the meaning of red ocean is being reproduced here.

A red ocean market is a highly competitive market in which there are many established players are vying for the same customers and resources and the market is saturated. The term "red ocean" is used to describe this market because the market is depicted as a metaphorical "ocean" that is "red" with the blood of the companies that are competing in the market. In this type of market, businesses need to compete on price, features, and other traditional factors in order to differentiate themselves from their competitors and win market share. Businesses that exist in the Red ocean market scenario benefit immensely from strategy approach rather than unplanned arbitrary management approach. All things being equal, smarter, well organized and resourceful businesses are able to survive and manage to grow and increase their market share. Let us turn our attention some of the key strategies that businesses existing in Red ocean engage in order survive and grow their business.

## Sales strategies for competing in a red ocean market

What are the marketing and sales strategies for competing in a red ocean market scenario?

Ensuring Product Differentiation is paramount for any business. Businesses may differentiate their products or services from those of their competitors to stand out in the market. This may involve offering unique features, design or branding besides providing benefits, or positioning the product or service in a specific niche within the market. Price strategy to increase competitiveness in the market is an effective strategy that many businesses and brands engage in order to increase market share.

For achieving Cost competitiveness and Cost leadership businesses focus on design optimization ,innovation, product development ,value engineering initiatives to improve the product design and functionalities and thereby reduce the price of the end product on 'a value for money' proposition while the business is able maintain the profitability on the particular product . These initiatives may also involve streamlining operations, reducing waste, and evolving new and more robust operating and business models

Innovation and Customer centricity is paramount for any business or brand. Through the process of innovation brands may focus on creating a solution that perfectly solves the latent problem faced by the customers and in this way businesses engage innovation perpetually in order to introduce new products or services that meet the evolving needs of their customers.

Brands may focus on providing excellent customer service and building strong relationships with their customers in order to differentiate themselves from their competitors and build loyalty. Providing excellent customer service can help companies to stand out in a red ocean market, as it can help create a positive customer experience and foster strong customer relationship and loyalty.

Businesses engage in strategic collaboration ,business tie ups, joint ventures with other potential organizations which are synergistic and complimentary to the business in order to access new markets or geographies and thus increase the customer footprint.

Businesses engage unique branding and sales promotion initiatives that provide a novelty and freshness to the campaign and a certain focus on the exact audience with in the red ocean who are more likely to prefer the brand over the competitors.

It's important for Businesses operating in the Red ocean market place to continuously assess and adjust their marketing and sales strategies in order to stay competitive. This may involve evaluating the effectiveness of current strategies and testing new approaches to continuously evaluate and implement action that works best for the business.

**Blue Ocean Strategy**

While tracing through the journey of entrepreneurship in disruptive marketing approaches let us look at one relevant concept namely blue ocean strategy and how the initiative was engaged by businesses to scale their business revenues and create brand leaders.

Blue ocean strategy is a business approach that involves creating new markets and value for customers, rather than competing in existing markets. This approach involves identifying untapped market opportunities and creating products or services that meet the needs of these new markets. One of the key principles of blue ocean strategy is to look beyond the traditional boundaries of the industry in which a company operates and to seek out new opportunities for growth. Companies that follow a blue ocean strategy seek to create value for customers in ways that are not offered by their competitors, and they aim to create a unique value proposition that sets them apart in the market.

Let us look at the Examples of successful businesses that have employed a blue ocean strategy to create brand leadership in their respective fields.

Apple: Apple has consistently disrupted existing markets and created new ones through the introduction of innovative products, such as the iPod, iPhone, and iPad, that meet the needs of customers in new and innovative ways.

Tesla: Tesla has disrupted the traditional automotive industry by introducing electric vehicles that offer a unique value proposition and meet the needs of customers thereby revolutionizing the automobile industry.

Netflix: Netflix has disrupted the traditional television and film industries by offering a subscription-based streaming service that allows users to watch movies and TV shows on demand. This innovative business model allowed Netflix to create a new market and different value proposition for customers.

Airbnb: Airbnb has disrupted the traditional hotel industry by offering a platform that allows individuals to rent out their homes or apartments to travelers. This innovative business model allowed Airbnb to create a new market and value proposition for customers.

**Disruptive business models and strategies**

In order to understand how businesses created different business models and strategies thus disrupted the previously existing business model in the particular industry and the particular market. We will commence the discussion with the Zara Brand of apparels.

Zara, a Spanish fast fashion brand disrupted the traditional apparel industry by offering a wide range of trendy, high-quality clothing at affordable prices. The brand succeeded in establishing itself as a leading global apparel brand by adopting the following strategies, namely:

Vertical integration: Zara implemented a vertical integration business model, which means that the company controlled every stage of the production process, from design to distribution. This allowed Zara to respond to changing trends and customer demands on real time basis.

Fast fashion: Zara embraced the concept of fast fashion, which involved quickly production and distribution of new styles in response to fast growing changing trends. This allowed the company to continually refresh its product offerings and keep the customers engaged thereby producing exponentiality in Sales.

In-house design and production: Zara created a robust in-house design team responsible for continuously creating new styles and trends. The company also created its own production facilities, which allowed it to ensure consistency in product quality and greater control over the its inventory.

Strong branding: Zara developed a strong brand identity through its focus on fashion and design. The company also invested in marketing campaigns to promote its brand and products.

Global expansion: Zara aggressively expanded its global presence through the establishment of stores in major cities around the world. The company also implemented e-commerce and direct-to-consumer sales strategies to reach customers online.

Overall in a summary it can be concluded that , Zara's revenue scalability and exponential growth and business success can be attributed to its focus on vertical integration, fast fashion, in-house design and production, strong branding, and global expansion. These strategies have allowed the company to disrupt the traditional apparel industry and establish itself as a leading global brand.

In order to validate our understanding on the strategies that played a role in the success of the Zara brand , we may understand how the business model adopted by Zara was different from the traditional apparel brands which Zara eventually disrupted?

Traditionally, apparel brands functioned with a horizontal integration based business model, which involved outsourcing various stages of the production process to different suppliers or job work -manufacturers. In essence the model was cost-effective, but as it was decentralized it posed huge challenges and the system was slower and less responsive to be able to adopt to changing trends and customer demands.

In contrast, Zara implemented a vertical integration business model, which meant that the company controlled every stage of the production process, from design to distribution. This allowed Zara to respond quickly to changing trends and customer demands and produce new styles and trends on a fast fashion cycle.

Overall in summary , the main difference between the traditional apparel business model and the model used by Zara was the level of control that the company has over the production process. Traditional apparel brands relied on outsourcing various stages of production, while Zara opted for a more integrated approach that allowed it to have greater control over the quality and timeliness of its products. This allowed Zara to disrupt the traditional apparel industry and establish itself as a leading global brand.

**More Disruptive strategies**

Let us look at another example of how an Indian business adopted a different strategy that produced huge scalability which caused a disruption in the Indian paint industry?

Asian Paints a leading Indian paint company disrupted the paint market by eliminating intermediaries such as distributors and dealing directly with retail shops. This has allowed the company to reduce costs and improve efficiency by cutting out an unnecessary layer in the supply chain. It has also given the company more control over its distribution network and has allowed it to more effectively target and serve its customers.

In addition, Asian Paints invested in a robust market intelligence framework to better understand the needs and preferences of its customers. This includes gathering and analyzing data on consumer behavior, market trends, and competitor information. By using this information, the company has been able to develop products and services that better meet the needs of its customers and stay ahead of competitors. Overall, Asian Paints' strategy of eliminating distributors and dealing directly with retail shops and investment in market intelligence helped the company to disrupt the paint market and maintain its position as a leader in the industry.

# CHAPTER ELEVEN

# PRODUCT ECOSYSTEM

Let us understand the meaning of product ecosystem from the point of marketing strategy?

Creation of 'product ecosystem' another strategy namely which resulted in the creation of new market paradigms that brands engaged for business scalability and exponential sales growth cross selling and upselling and creating a large loyal and perpetual customer base producing brand leadership and huge value creation.

A product ecosystem is a network of products, services, and other resources that are related to a specific product or product line. The concept of a product ecosystem can be helpful for businesses because it provides a holistic view of the various elements that contribute to the success of a product.

In other words, a product ecosystem is a network of interconnected products, services, and other elements that support and enhance the value of a particular product or service.

From the point of view of marketing strategy, a product ecosystem can be used to create additional value for customers, differentiate a product from competitors, and create new revenue streams for the business through cross selling ,upselling and thus expand the life time value of the client and the revenue per customer.

A product ecosystem strategy can help a business to increase sales in several ways. For example, by understanding the various components of the product ecosystem, a business can identify opportunities to expand its product offerings and create new revenue streams. This might include introducing complementary products or services, or partnering with other companies to offer bundled products or services.

For example, a smartphone manufacturer may create a product ecosystem around its smartphone products by offering a range of accessories, such as cases, chargers, and headphones. These accessories can enhance the value of the smartphone for customers and create additional revenue streams for the manufacturer.

Another example of a product ecosystem is a software company that offers a range of products and services that complement its core software product. For example, the company may offer training, support, consulting, and integrations to help customers get the most out of its software. These additional products and services can help the company differentiate itself from competitors and create a more comprehensive solution for its customers and in turn contribute to huge revenue scalability.

In addition, a product ecosystem strategy can help a business to improve customer loyalty and retention by providing a more comprehensive and integrated product experience. By offering a range of products and services that work together seamlessly, a business can create a more compelling value proposition for its customers.

Overall, the concept of a product ecosystem can be a useful tool for businesses looking to increase sales by expanding their product offerings, improving customer loyalty and retention, and creating new revenue streams.

Let us understand the example of Apple who is one of the foremost brands that succeeded in creating a product ecosystem concept to increase sales revenues and exponential growth

Apple has created a product ecosystem by developing a range of interconnected products and services that work together seamlessly and offer a comprehensive user experience. This ecosystem approach has helped the company to increase sales revenues per customer by encouraging customers to purchase multiple products and services from Apple and to use them in combination with one another. For example, Apple's ecosystem includes hardware products such as the iPhone, iPad, Mac, and Apple Watch, as well as software products like the iOS operating system, macOS, and various productivity and creativity apps. These products are designed to work together and offer a consistent user experience across different devices.

In addition, Apple offers a range of services, including the App Store, iTunes Store, iCloud, and Apple Music, which are all designed to be used in conjunction with its hardware products. By offering a wide range of products and services that work together, Apple is able to create a cohesive user experience and encourage customers to purchase multiple products and services from the company. Overall, Apple's product ecosystem approach has been a key part of the company's success and has helped to drive sales revenues by encouraging customers to purchase multiple products and use them in combination with one another.

It will serve the discussion to understand four recognized worldwide brands which have effectively leveraged the concept of Ecosystem to scale their business and achieve brand leadership in their respective field :

Microsoft: Microsoft has created a product ecosystem around its Windows operating system and Office software by offering a range of products and services, such as Azure cloud computing, Dynamics CRM, and LinkedIn.

Amazon: Amazon has created a product ecosystem around its e-commerce platform by offering a range of products and services, such as Amazon Prime, Amazon Web Services, and Amazon Advertising.

Google: Google has created a product ecosystem around its search and advertising products by offering a range of products and services, such as Google Maps, Google Drive, and Google Ads.

Samsung: Samsung has created a product ecosystem around its smartphones and other electronics products by offering a range of accessories and services, such as the Samsung Pay mobile payment platform and the Samsung Health fitness tracker.

# CHAPTER TWELVE

# LEVERAGING CHANGE IN THE MARKETPLACE

We have seen that number of businesses have leveraged changes in the market place to fuel their growth and establish themselves as leaders in their respective industries. let us take the example of the following five Indian businesses that have leveraged change in the market place to craft their business growth and revenue scalability.

Flipkart an Indian e-commerce company founded in 2007 managed to leverage the manifold growth in the online shopping market in India to become one of the leading e-commerce companies in the country. Flipkart has implemented strategies such as offering a wide range of products, providing excellent customer service, and implementing a strong delivery network to fuel its growth.

Oyo: Oyo is an Indian hospitality company founded in 2013 leveraged the growth of the travel and tourism industry in India to become one of the leading hotel chains in the country. Oyo has implemented strategies such as offering a wide range of accommodation options, utilizing technology to streamline operations, and expanding internationally to fuel its growth.

Swiggy: Swiggy is an Indian food delivery company founded in 2014 leveraged the growth of the online food delivery market in India to become one of the leading food delivery companies in the country. Swiggy has implemented strategies such as offering a wide range of food options, utilizing technology to streamline operations, and expanding internationally to fuel its growth.

Paytm: Paytm is an Indian digital payments company that was founded in 2010. The company has leveraged the growth of the digital payments market in India to become one of the leading digital payments companies in the country. Paytm has implemented strategies such as offering a wide range of payment options, utilizing technology to streamline operations, and expanding internationally to fuel its growth.

Ola: Ola is an Indian ride-hailing company that was founded in 2010. The company has leveraged the growth of the ride-hailing market in India to become one of the leading ride-hailing companies in the country. Ola has implemented strategies such as offering a wide range of transportation options, utilizing technology to streamline operations, and expanding internationally to fuel its growth.

In the succeeding lines we will examine the marketing strategies of the following five successful brands who derived huge value and created sales scalability

**Key strategies engaged by Microsoft**

Let us understand the marketing strategies that Microsoft has adopted which helped the business to emerge as the brand leader in the tech field:

Microsoft's success has been built on four core strategies which include continuous product innovation, strategic partnerships and acquisitions, marketing and promotion campaigns, and a strong customer support as follows:

Product diversification: Microsoft has a wide range of products and services, including operating systems, productivity software, gaming consoles, and cloud services, which have helped the company reach a diverse customer base and maintain its market leadership.

Strategic Partnerships and acquisitions: Microsoft has also made strategic partnerships and acquisitions to expand its reach and capabilities. For example, the company has partnered with other technology/ firms to develop new products and services, and it has acquired companies to gain access to new technologies and markets.

Marketing campaigns: Microsoft has invested heavily in marketing campaigns to promote its products and build brand awareness. The company has used various marketing channels, including television commercials, social media, and online advertising, to reach its target audience.

Customer support: Microsoft has also focused on providing excellent customer support to retain customers and maintain its reputation. The company has a dedicated team of customer support representatives who are available to help customers with any issues or questions they may have.

## Key strategies engaged by Asian Paints

As the second example let us look at the key strategies employed by Asian Paints to consistently grow sales revenue and deliver high profitability

Asian Paints is one of the leading paint companies in India and has consistently grown its sales revenue and delivered high profitability through a combination of strategies, including:

Diversification of products and services: The company has diversified its product portfolio to include a range of paints, coatings, and home improvement products and services, which has helped the company to tap into new market segments and drive sales growth.

Expansion into new markets: the company has pursued an aggressive expansion strategy, entering new markets both within India and internationally, which has helped the company to reach new geographies and exponentially grow revenues.

Innovation: The company has invested in market intelligence which has helped the business to have an in-depth understanding of the market dynamics and thus increase the market share. The Company has invested heavily in research and development in the field to introduce new and innovative products and technologies, which has helped the company to stay ahead of competitors and drive sales growth.

Strong distribution network: Having removed the tier of distributors the company in turn directly deal with the retailers across the country and in other markets.

Marketing and branding: The company employed effective marketing and branding strategies to build product awareness and establish a strong brand identity in the market.

**Key strategies engaged by Amul**

As the third example let us understand the core revenue scalability strategy adopted by Amul to become a market leader

Amul is an Indian dairy cooperative that has become a market leader in the country through a combination of innovative business practices, effective marketing, and a focus on quality and customer satisfaction.

One key element of Amul's growth strategy has been the development of a decentralized, cooperative business model that empowers local farmers and encourages them to invest in the success of the company. This model has helped Amul to build a strong base of loyal customers and to secure a steady supply of high-quality milk and other dairy products.

In addition, Amul has employed effective marketing strategies to build brand awareness and customer loyalty. The company has used catchy slogans and memorable advertisements to promote its products and has also engaged with consumers through social media and other channels.

Amul has also placed a strong emphasis on quality and customer satisfaction, consistently delivering high-quality products and offering excellent customer service. This focus on quality has helped the company to build a strong reputation and to maintain its position as a market leader.

Overall, Amul's growth strategy has been built on a combination of innovative business practices, effective marketing, and a focus on quality and customer satisfaction, which have all contributed to the company's success and helped it to become a market leader.

**Key strategies engaged by Amazon**

As the third example let us understand the core revenue scalability strategy adopted by Amazon to get ahead of competition?

Amazon has been able to get ahead of the competition through a combination of strategies, namely innovation, customer satisfaction, diversification, global expansion, and building a strong brand, the details are as hereunder:

Innovation: Amazon has consistently invested in research and development to introduce new and innovative products and services. This includes the development of new technologies, such as the Amazon Web Services cloud computing platform, and the expansion into new markets, such as e-commerce, digital media, and advertising.

Customer focus: Amazon has placed a strong emphasis on customer satisfaction and has consistently worked to improve the customer experience. This includes offering a wide selection of products, competitive prices, fast and convenient delivery options, and excellent customer service.

Diversification: Amazon has diversified its product and service offerings, expanding beyond its core e-commerce business into areas such as cloud computing, digital media, and advertising. This has helped the company to reach new customers and tap into new revenue streams.

Global expansion: Amazon has pursued an aggressive expansion strategy, entering new markets around the world and establishing a presence in a wide range of countries. This has helped the company to reach a global customer base and capture a larger share of the market.

Strong brand: Amazon has also built a strong brand identity, establishing itself as a trusted and reliable source for online shopping. This has helped the company to attract and retain customers, as well as to command premium prices for its products and services

As the fourth example let us look at example of Nike brand a global apparel and footwear company and the specific marketing strategies which helped the company to grow its sales and consistently demonstrated strong revenues and exponential growth

Building strong brands: Nike has built a strong brand through its focus on quality, innovation, and design. The company has also invested in marketing campaigns to promote its brand and products.

Expanding distribution: Nike has expanded its distribution network to reach customers in more markets around the world. The company has also implemented strategies such as e-commerce and direct-to-consumer sales to reach customers online.

Collaborating with influencers and athletes: Nike has collaborated with influencers and athletes to promote its products and build brand awareness. The company has also sponsored events and teams to reach new audiences.

Investing in research and development: Nike has invested in research and development to continually improve its products and stay ahead of the competition. The company has also implemented sustainability initiatives to reduce its environmental impact and contribute to the well-being of the communities in which it operates.

**Key strategies engaged by Zoho**

As the fifth example let us study the key strategies engaged by Zoho to deliver high business growth and revenue scalability to become a unicorn

Zoho is a software company that has achieved high business growth and revenue scalability to become a unicorn through a combination of strategies, including

Diversification of products and services: Zoho has developed a wide range of software products and services that cater to different industries and market segments, which has helped the company to achieve high business growth by reaching a diverse customer base.

Focus on customer satisfaction: Zoho has placed a strong emphasis on customer satisfaction, consistently delivering high-quality products and services and offering excellent customer support. This focus on customer satisfaction has helped the company to build a loyal customer base and drive revenue growth.

Innovation: Zoho has invested heavily in research and development to introduce new and innovative products and technologies, which has helped the company to stay ahead of competitors and drive revenue growth.

Marketing and branding: Zoho has employed effective marketing and branding strategies to build awareness of its products and to establish a strong brand identity in the market.

Strong partnerships and collaborations: Zoho has formed partnerships and collaborations with other companies and organizations to expand its reach and drive revenue growth.

It is evident from the five aforementioned examples as to how businesses have devised similar and distinguishing strategy approaches that have helped the brands to create extraordinary revenue growth and scalability.

# CHAPTER THIRTEEN

# CUSTOMER OBSESSION

Let us understand the relevance of customer acquisition strategy and Customer Retention strategy in basic terms?

Customer acquisition and customer retention are both important strategies for businesses seeking to grow and succeed. Customer acquisition involves attracting and converting new customers, while customer retention involves keeping existing customers loyal and engaged. A customer acquisition strategy typically involves identifying and targeting potential customers, developing marketing and sales efforts to attract them, and converting them into paying customers. This may involve using a variety of tactics, such as advertising, promotions, and public relations, as well as developing and nurturing relationships with potential customers.

On the other hand, a customer retention strategy focuses on keeping existing customers satisfied and loyal to the business. This may involve providing excellent customer service, offering incentives and rewards for repeat business, and continuously improving and evolving the product or service offering to meet the changing needs and preferences of customers. By prioritizing customer retention, businesses can reduce the costs and effort associated with acquiring new customers and build long-term, profitable relationships.

In order to understand the above we will turn our attention to a very basic practical illustration of customer acquisition and retention strategies:

A small clothing retailer is looking to grow its business and increase sales. The retailer develops a customer acquisition strategy that includes targeted online advertising campaigns and in-store promotions to attract new customers. The retailer also collaborates with local fashion bloggers and influencers to promote its products and establish a presence in the community. As a result of these efforts, the retailer is able to attract a number of new customers and increase its sales.

However, the retailer recognizes that it is also important to focus on customer retention in order to sustain its growth and success. To this end, the retailer implements a customer retention strategy that includes providing excellent customer service, offering a loyalty rewards program, and regularly soliciting customer feedback and using it to improve the shopping experience. These efforts help to keep the retailer's existing customers happy and loyal, and contribute to the overall growth and success of the business.

**Customer Retention strategies and Customer obsession**

Let us understand the relevance of Customer Retention strategies and Customer obsession?

Customer obsession is the new and the eternal pursuit for organized businesses. In a market place filled with multiple vendors and suppliers for virtually all type of products brand loyalty as a distinct factor provides the most important value.

Each and every business and Brand seeks to stay relevant vying with each other with all the right actions to make the customer the center point and pouring their attention on the customer.

The following are some of the key aspects that businesses address through the customer retention strategy:

Aligning the product service or the solution to address the need of the customer, Continuously deliver value to the customer through multifaceted and perpetual actions meant to deliver higher and higher customer experience, Improving the customer experience from the prospecting stage right up to the delivery and feedback stage, Delivering quality with non-negotiable product return facility for customer thereby to earn the customer loyalty and perpetual customer engagement, Robust Post order coordination processes internally between the sales department and the operations and delivery department to track and ensure timely delivery and consistent quality, Customer engagement post-delivery via feedback and testimonials and taking corrective steps , filling the lacuna by learning from mistakes.

As part of the customer retention strategy business constitute independent back end resource or even team entrusted with customer engagement related quality assurance and continually tracking customer feedback and obsessing on the customer gauging his satisfaction quotient. And Customers obviously like that extra attention and the brand gets the recall in the end bargain.

This in turn gives the brand the advantage of large pool of customers, ensuring Sales revenue growth and consistency and a steady buildup of new customer month after month and ensuring multiple and perpetual transactions from existing customers with an impressive loyalty chain buildup.

What is the relevance of customer obsession in the new world order?

Is the obsession of many successful SMB businesses in increased engagement with the customer even to the point which could be termed as obsessive behavior really justified? can the SMB business afford this stance?

To examine the above question we need to see the other side of the world with clear perspective ?

In a market place that is filled with multiple players offering the similar products within a user class and many of them being more advantaged in terms of being older players with an established brand and customers for a business player ensuring business survival and growth in sales is extremely challenging.

All SMB businesses which have limitation in the capital that they can deploy in their respective business realize certain very important and salient irrefutable facts which are as follows:

a) High Cost of business or customer acquisition

b) There are both tangible and intangible cost of sustaining business.

c) Relatively high Opportunity cost of losing an existing paying customer.

d) One key or major customer lost is virtually like an industry vertical lost.

e) Business have high Vulnerabilities to new players and competition

f) Closing the door for competitor -theory practiced by businesses limit opportunities for new customer acquisition.

It is evident that there is a premium around both acquiring a customer and losing a customer. Customer retention is extremely important for businesses to survive and grow their businesses. And in their way forward, businesses realize that aligning their products and solutions to meet the needs of the customer and even changing customer perceptions and expectations makes strategic sense in the long run.

In this manner, through continuously delivering value to the end customer and constantly engaging with the customer both before and after the sale transaction creates a certain loyalty and connect with the brand that is fortified by consistent and reliable delivery, customer friendly product return and replacement policy, after service response to customer queries and so on.

In their pursuit for retaining market share and growing the customer fraternity, businesses practice behavior that manifest customer obsession, and some of them use the following approach:

a) Using technology to capture every aspect of the customer engagement in minute detail with a track on the customer footprint and customer behavior.

(b) Profiling customer and building relationships by adopting appropriate engagement models.

(c) Continuous Innovation and product development to offer better value to existing client based on customer feedback, customer complaints.

Customer retention strategies and obsessive customer engagements recognize that an existing client is a piece of intangible value in the books of accounts, the longer the customer is with the brand it is likely to create and continuously adds enterprise value, while validating the products and services offered by the business.

With the above backdrop we will examine the actual scenario in the SMB perspective at the other end of the spectrum:

A large number of SMB businesses do not ensure robust preorder stage processes nor a proper post order execution delivery processes which provides a hassle free experience to the end customer. This leads to ordeals for the customer from the initial preorder customer engagement stage.

Lack of systems and processes in the post order stage results in recurrence of delayed deliveries, non-adherence to critical schedules, repetitive quality issues at the last hour, stringent product return policies, accentuated by their apathy and lack of attention to customer complaints and feedback, in general weak customer response processes, so on and so forth.

This causes serious doubts in the mind of the customer as a result of which that business is most likely to lose it share of business within that customer account.

And in all probability the above scenario could potentially pave the way for a rival competitor to enter the same customer account and substitute the business or product.

In a market place where there is stiff competition in terms of multiple vendors, competitors who are targeting the same client as well as the same order , any shortcoming on account of any one or more of the above aspects enumerated above can potentially cause the business to lose the order and the customer.

If the situation remain uncorrected within these SMB businesses over a protracted period of time, then such businesses slowly lose grip of the market while their regular ,Loyal and key customers accounts desert the business moving to their rival and competitor businesses.

As a result of serious lack of sales these SMB businesses face negative cash flows and severe cash crunch. Many of these businesses are eventually forced to disband their sales team which was built by them over the years painstakingly over the years incurring money and time. These SMB businesses are on their way to a potential business failure.

But ironically, after the occurrence of the business failure, the entrepreneurs managing these SMB businesses in their introspective analysis of the causes for their business failure, they are more likely to blame the industry trends, or the market recession or any other miscellaneous factors as the principle reason for their business failure very often not realizing the factors that were not managed and which were entirely in their control.

# CHAPTER FOURTEEN

# BUSINESS MODEL

Coming from the discussion regarding sales strategies, Let us understand the term Business Model.

A business model is a framework that outlines how a business organization creates, delivers, and captures value. It describes the products or services that a company offers, the target customer segments that the company serves, the channels through which the company reaches those customers, and the resources and partners that the company needs to create and deliver its products or services. A business model also describes the sources of revenue that a company generates and the costs that it incurs in order to create and deliver value to its customers.

This understanding brings up the question: what is the difference between business model and operating model?

An operating model, on the other hand, refers to the way in which a company organizes and coordinates its resources and processes in order to deliver its products or services. An operating model describes the specific roles, responsibilities, and processes that are used to create and deliver value to customers. It also outlines the systems, technologies, and infrastructure that a company uses to support its operations.

Overall, the business model describes how a company creates and delivers value to its customers, while the operating model describes how the company organizes and coordinates its resources and processes to deliver that value.

## Change in Business model

Do business model's change as businesses evolve?

Through the forgoing we have understood the terms in all its dimensions particularly that Business model is essentially the way in which a business dealing in products and services engage with end clients across all the possible avenues within a market place. For illustration it may be said that a business may be pursuing 'direct selling to customer',or Channel Sales (B2B2C) 'Selling to customer through channel partner' as a second option and Selling to customer through online avenues(B2C) as another option ,and engaging with customers by identifying customers through tender (B2B ) and so on, as the case may be.

Depending on the type of business a 'business model' is evolved in such a way that the business is able to engage with the customer in other words acquire and retain customers producing the envisaged growth and scalability for the business and satisfactory customer experience for the customer. The right business model helps the business to attain the full potential for its products and services in terms of the available opportunities within the specific geography or generally the Territory.

Thus Business Model become the pivot of the sales strategy formulation process. Designing the business model and redefining the business model from time to time as and when necessary as the business is passing or growing through its life cycle in relationship with the market place.

Redefining the business model may become necessary with the passing times in order to streamline and optimize sales and thus produce consistent Sales revenue growth. This is clearly the responsibility of the sales department and the corporate management of any Business Entity.

Creation of the Business model ensures alignment with the other core business functions like Operations, Delivery, Finance and validation of the achievability of sales goals.

For a just started business, the entrepreneur understands the business model in a certain way and engages with the customers accordingly. Within a short period of time as their understanding and experience with the customers and the players operating in the market increases they feel that the business model now needs alteration and that that business model will not serve the internet off the business rather it will be limiting the growth of sales of the business. So the entrepreneur carves a new business model with the available information and their new found experience even understanding other peer businesses and creating the new business model.

When the entrepreneur is not coming from the right clarity they consider the change in business model with great apprehension and take the need for change as a sign of adversity or a mistake.

In reality, it is to be understood that change in business model is a reflection of the business passing through growth thresholds and in reality that through iterations businesses finally end up discovering the business model which works best for the business given their strengths and their limitations, so changes in business model which serve the interest of the business is part of the growth process.

To understand this imperative for businesses to reinvent their business model in the course of their business evolution we may examine the following illustration of the following four Indian businesses which grew by changing their business model to leverage growth

Flipkart: Flipkart an Indian e-commerce company founded in 2007 initially operated as an online marketplace, connecting buyers and sellers. However, in order to fuel its growth and exponentially scale the business Flipkart changed its business model to become an online retailer, offering its own products as well as a wide range of products fulfilling orders directly to customers.

Oyo: Oyo an Indian hospitality company founded in 2013. The company initially operated as an online marketplace, connecting hotel owners with travelers. However, perceiving business opportunities, Oyo changed its business model to become an online hotel chain, offering its own branded accommodation options and controlling the entire customer experience. This change allowed Oyo to offer a wider range of accommodation options, improve the quality of its offerings, and control the customer experience, which helped fuel its growth.

Swiggy: Swiggy an Indian food delivery company founded in 2014 initially operated as an online marketplace, connecting restaurants with customers. However, have observed business opportunities Swiggy changed its business model to become a food delivery company, offering its own delivery services and controlling the entire delivery process. This change allowed Swiggy to offer a wider range of food options, improve the delivery experience, and control the fulfillment process, which helped fuel its huge business growth.

Paytm: Paytm an Indian digital payments company founded in 2010 initially operated as a mobile recharge and utility payments platform. However, understood the space and perceiving opportunities Paytm changed its business model to become a full-service digital payments platform, offering a wide range of payment options and expanding into other areas such as e-commerce and financial services. This change allowed Paytm to offer a wider range of payment options, improve the customer experience, and control the fulfillment process, which helped fuel its growth.

# CHAPTER FIFTEEN

# SALES STRATEGIES AND FINANCIAL MANAGEMENT LINKAGES

There is a direct connection between Sales strategies and Financial management, in this context let us understand the following concepts and terms which are commonly referred in to in the context of marketing and sales which has a financial implication:

**Client Acquisition Cost**

What is the meaning of client acquisition cost?

Client acquisition cost (CAC) refers to the amount of money that a business spends on acquiring a new customer. This includes all of the costs associated with attracting and converting potential customers into paying customers. These costs can include marketing expenses, sales expenses, and any other expenses incurred in the process of acquiring new customers.

The CAC can be a useful metric for businesses to track and understand, as it can help them to determine the efficiency of their customer acquisition efforts and the overall profitability of their business. By understanding the CAC, businesses can make informed decisions about where to allocate their resources and how much they can afford to spend on acquiring new customers.

To calculate the CAC, you can divide the total amount spent on acquiring new customers over a specific period of time (e.g. a month or a year) by the number of new customers acquired during that period. This will give you the average CAC per customer.

This can be useful information for the business, as it allows them to compare the CAC to the lifetime value (LTV) of their customers to determine the overall profitability of their customer acquisition efforts.

So, the point that needs to be emphasized is that the cost of business acquisition will be different across the various sales avenues that we have seen in the preceding paragraphs.

In other words, the acquisition cost in the case of direct sales to customer may be different from the cost that is incurred when the business sells through the channels. Similarly, the business acquisition cost through online will be different as compared to direct sales. Similarly, acquiring business through the process of tendering may be lesser than the channel sales.

Businesses need to keep a real-time track of the sales acquisition cost for sourcing sales under each and every business avenue. Like all cost this needs to be tracked, analyzed and optimized and kept at the need level.

In order to keep the business acquisition cost at an optimum level through the process of averaging and broad basing the cost, businesses need to address all the possible sales avenues for acquiring and growing their sales .In this way the aggregate cost of acquiring business and the sales overheads will be maintained at the budgeted level.

For Businesses which inherently are limited to solely one avenue, for meeting the imperative to continuously grow sales , increase product volumes, and also augment number of customers from period to period basis, while balancing with financial capacity, the business acquisition cost need to be tracked and kept in check, in order to contain the cost at the desirable budgeted level.

## Lifetime value of a client

Let us understand another term namely ' life time value of a client' with the following question:

What is the meaning of life time value of a client? how does it impact profit? what must businesses do to increase life time value of a client?

The lifetime value (LTV) of a customer refers to the total value of sales from a particular customer over the course of their relationship with the business and the product concerned. It is calculated by multiplying the average amount of money that a customer spends per purchase by the number of purchases that the customer is expected to make over their lifetime.

The LTV of a customer can impact profit in several ways. For example, if a business has a high LTV, it may be able to spend more on marketing and sales efforts to acquire new customers, since the long-term value of those customers is expected to be higher.

Higher LTV will mean higher profitability for the business as the business is able to have an increasing number of customers with higher LTV the marketing and sales budgets can be optimized and limited with more financial prudence. For a growing business higher LTV of many customers help the business to engage its marketing budget towards acquiring new customers and produce exponentially in sales revenues. Businesses put in place customer retention strategies that promote greater brand engagement, better customer experience all of which contribute to long term client relationship and higher lifetime value per client.

Businesses also have the advantage of devising pricing strategies along with discounts and schemes in order to produce greater business traction and while being able to garner more profit even without losing sight of the need to provide the customer with the 'value for money'.Many businesses with high LTV customers may be able to charge higher prices or offer more premium products or services, since their customers are willing to pay more for those offerings.

Let us summarize some of the steps that may be adopted by a business in order to increase the LTV of a customer:

Providing excellent customer service: By consistently providing high-quality customer service, businesses can build strong relationships with their customers and increase the likelihood that those customers will continue to do business with the company.

Offering a wide range of products or services: By offering a diverse range of products or services, businesses can appeal to a wider customer base and increase the likelihood that customers will continue to do business with the company over time.

Implementing loyalty programs: Loyalty programs can incentivize customers to continue doing business with a company by offering rewards or discounts for repeat purchases.

Personalizing the customer experience: By personalizing the customer experience, businesses can create a more tailored and engaging experience for their customers, which can increase the likelihood that those customers will continue to do business with the company.

## Role of financial management in driving Sales Growth

Let us look at an important aspect namely 'The Role of financial management in driving Sales growth.

Strategic business goals need to be validated from a financial perspective even before they are adopted by the business as a sacrosanct number. Financial principles and perspective are equally important to be considered while formulating business strategies.

In other words, it is important for businesses to carefully consider the financial implications of their strategic revenue goals and ensure that they are viable and sustainable from a financial perspective. This can help to ensure that the business is able to effectively execute its plans and strategies and achieve their business Goals.

Intervention with financial implications such as product pricing, cost management, and working capital management are part of the financial strategies of any business. These strategic aspects are capable of contributing to sales growth and scalability and higher profitability.

Strategic pricing of products and services is crucial for ensuring that the business is able to generate more business traction , ensure market competitiveness , provide value for the customers money and achieve sufficient revenue to cover its costs and achieve envisaged profitability.

Cost management involves minimizing expenses and maximizing efficiency in order to increase profitability. Effective working capital management, which involves managing the business's short-term financial resources, such as cash and inventory, is also essential for ensuring the financial health and stability of the business. By addressing these factors and implementing sound financial management practices, businesses are able to optimize their financial performance while being able to achieve sales growth.

Many businesses engage robust financial processes and tools for accurately forecasting Sales and creating budgets for sales expenses and marketing promo budgets and implement financial checks and balances along with financial Reviews for allocating resources effectively, and continuously monitoring and analyzing financial performance.

By aligning financial strategies with the business's overall goals and objectives, financial management can help to optimize sales growth and drive success.

## Fixing Credit policies for credit businesses

Why should SMB businesses fix credit policies to manage their credit business and mitigate financial risk of non-payment by customers?

Businesses that are against credit, or that have a policy of not extending credit to their customers, typically have systems and processes in place to manage their business in this way. Some ways that businesses can fix credit policies to manage their business against credit include:

Businesses can effectively manage their business against credit and reduce the risk of non-payment or late payment from customers. It's important for businesses to carefully evaluate the risks and benefits of extending credit, and to develop policies that are aligned with their overall business goals and objectives.

Intrinsically, the most preferred payment terms for businesses is payment against Cash or in other words 'Cash and Carry' terms. This can help businesses to avoid the financial risk of non-payment or late payment from customers. Businesses can also offer alternative payment options, such as debit or credit card payments, online payments, or electronic payment systems, to make it easier for customers to pay for products or services without extending credit.

Businesses need to offer discounts or other incentives to customers who pay upfront, in order to encourage them to choose this payment option.

In case of credit business where there is an established practice in the particular industry businesses need to fix credit policies in other words establish clear payment terms, such as deadlines for payment, late payment fees, or other penalties, in order to encourage prompt payment and manage against credit. Further, Businesses need to implement credit checks on potential customers in order to assess their creditworthiness .

## Price chart and standard Payment policies

What is the importance of price chart and standardization of payment terms? what is the necessity for formal price and payment terms approval prior to sending quotation or offer to a prospective customer?

In SMB businesses the ultimate decision regarding price and any last minute discount is taken by the founder entrepreneur so there is a possibility for lag or delay in submitting the sales offers to customers by the sales team.

The delay or the lag is caused on account of the need for obtaining the clearance to proceed and submit the quotation or close the order with the customer at a certain price even for the most regular product dealt with by the Business concerned...this ultimately becomes a limiting factor.

In some cases it sets a wrong impression in the mind of the customer and may negatively influence his decision.

As mentioned earlier in many SMB businesses the subject of pricing, and relevant terms and conditions is centralized at the founder MD level. Very often the sales department is able to derive the decisions on price and relevant terms only after multiple internal follow-ups.

No attempt is made to create a mechanism or standardize in terms of segregation of items for which price can be standardized and those which need internal assessment and analysis. This affects the response time of the business in conveying the pricing terms to the end customer.

It is also a fact that in the case of a large number of SMB businesses due to the general indecisiveness of the founder entrepreneur concerned, the price quotations are delayed .

Businesses fail to understand the imperative and the need for creating a formal pricing chart or price list, standardization of quotation structures formats covering standard terms and conditions to ensure speedy, responsive timeframes acceptable to customer prospects which in turn-increase the possibility of closing the customer's order.

These standardized documentation covering terms and other aspects need to be periodically reviewed and updated.

**Product Pricing strategy**

What is the importance of product pricing strategy and what are the different approaches in the formulation of the pricing strategy?

Strategic approach to dealing with pricing helps business to engage pricing as a tool for not only optimizing profitability but also use pricing for sales augmentation, increase market share, compete with peer competitor - businesses in the market and emerge winners thereon. But pricing strategy approaches will require the business to have solid processes for recording costs and reliable and sufficient data to provide the basis for making well informed strategy decisions.

It is clear that the pricing strategy should be aligned with the overall business strategy and take into account a variety of factors, such as the cost of producing the product, the target market, the competition, the price at which peer products or solutions are sold by competition and the value that the particular product provides to end customers. Business strategies regarding pricing cover five major aspects namely, cost related approach or competitor and market related approach, customer psychology related approach, premium positioning , discount based approach.

In cost-based pricing the business arrives at the price for the product after determining the cost of the producing the product the overhead and the profit is added to determine the price.

On the other hand in the case of Value-based pricing the business sets the price of the product based on the perceived value it provides to customers, rather than on the cost of producing the product.

In the case of Competitor based pricing or in other words 'Price Matching' the business sets the price of the product based on the prices of similar products offered by competitors in the market place.

This strategy can be effective if the business has a product or service that is comparable to the competitor's, and if the business is able to offer similar or better quality at a lower price.

In the case of Customer Psychology based pricing business sets the price of the product based on psychological factors, such as using certain price points that are perceived as more attractive to customers.

In the Premium positioning based pricing the business sets a high price for the product, positioning it as a luxury or high-end offering.

In the Discount based pricing the business sets a lower price for the product in order to increase sales revenues while reducing excess inventory and even attract price-sensitive customers to the brand.

Besides the above pricing approaches businesses engage the following pricing strategies for increasing sales revenue, growing exponentially and maximizing profitability and reducing inventory.

In the case of businesses which has created a unique product or service which is in high demand, or the business has a strong brand that commands a premium price businesses resorting to Price Skimming which involves setting a high initial price for the new innovative product offering and then gradually lowering the price over time as demand and competition increase.

In order to increase sale volumes in a short period businesses resort to Price undercutting namely offering a price that is significantly lower than the price of a competitor's product or service. This strategy can be effective if the business is able to offer a similar or better quality product or service at a lower price, and if it is able to offer more value to customers in other ways (e.g. through better customer service, faster delivery, etc.).

Bundle pricing involves offering a package deal to potential customers that includes multiple products or services at a discounted price. This strategy can be effective if the business is able to offer a bundle that is more attractive to customers than a competitor's similar bundle, or if it is able to offer a bundle that includes products or services that is not available to the customer from any other product source.

It needs to be borne in mind that businesses that engage Strategy approach in pricing are able to apply different approaches aforementioned in a dynamic manner depending on various factors and thus meet the business goals and objectives.

**Pricing processes and policies**

What are the direct impacts of lack of pricing processes and policies?

One of the biggest lacuna in SMB businesses is that many businesses inherently lack a standardized policy and a structured approach towards pricing decisions.

And very often there is lack of common direction as between the partners with regard to pricing decisions which directly affects the capacity of the business to convert sales prospects in to orders. The inconsistency in pricing is the result of a complete lack of a concrete pricing strategy or pricing policy invariably not documented, which otherwise could have been uniformly adopted by the team. This results in many ramifications some of the visible impacts are illustrated below:

Proposal and quotations are delayed because of lack of firm pricing policies and price standardization, leads to loss of business.

Loss of customers' orders to the rival competitors on account of perpetual delays in submission of quotations even though the business actually has superior products.

High level of arbitrariness and gut feel based pricing decisions do not secure envisaged profit target.

Inconsistency in pricing between the price offered by the business to its direct corporate customers and pricing for the same product when sold through dealers channels. This leads to loss of business as channel partners move to the competitors' products. Thereby causes loss of reputation and intern affects the brand credibility.

Internal conflicts between sales department and other departments on price related matters affects the business.

Loss of Competent people from the sales department as they are frustrated by wrong pricing policies.

**Deal ready with Pricing**

What are the steps to be taken by a business to be deal ready with regard to pricing and related payment terms and conditions ?

A business can create a speedy response system with regard to submission of quotations or proposals to the prospective customers if it can ensure the following aspects by creating a documented policy for the same namely : Price List, Terms and Conditions, payment terms ,credit policies, Price Revisions ,Discounts and Concessions etc.

In the case of SMB businesses after creating a policy frame work covering aforementioned aspects as and when there is need to secure a particular order where there are rival competitors bidding for the same orders if there is necessity for a downward revision in the price, the power to revise prices below the designated range or provide discounts to secure the order can be delegated to the director or the partner who is vested with the discretionary authority.

# CHAPTER SIXTEEN

# SALES DEPARTMENT – REALITIES AND CHALLENGES

Let us dwell on the different Questions faced by the Marketing sales function that commonly arise producing very conflicting angles ,alignments and correlation. But reflecting on these questions in the context of individual businesses is extremely important for the entrepreneur to be able to fix strategic goals and formulate strategies.

For a Business is a consistent sales growth an option?

It is matter of reality that more than two third of the businesses that fail are primarily on account of the business not being able to sell their goods or services to achieve the level of breakeven and profitability.

So the average SMB Business owner subsists in this fear of the potential loss of business or the uncertainty in terms of being able to acquire new business.

In most industry and business verticals the pace of change and disruption is so high that without the entrepreneur's knowledge the business itself is slowly losing relevance in the new business order that is setting in. And this gives rise to the substitution of one business in place of another business within the market place, one business failure directly gives rise to the uprising of another business, with the new business acquiring all the customers of the business which lost out.

The paradox of too much dependance on one customer?

The question really is : can you conclude that too much business from one customer is good for the business ? or is there need for risk mitigation?

For businesses certain customer accounts grow exponentially and by which the particular business or the brand becomes the principal vendor with continuous and perpetual orders. In a certain sense such customers become key customers and further such customer may contribute to more than 50 percent of the total sales for the particular year.

As the business engagement increase the dependance on the particular customer grows to the point where the organization is able to acquire new business without any perceptible marketing or sales effort. For some businesses this changes the entire perspective of the organization which was earlier marketing and sales centric is now moving to an operations and delivery centric business. In the medium term this business loses its core competencies which was the marketing and sales function given that some important sales resources have already left the business. This adversely affects the value of the brand.

Unknowingly, businesses become completely dependent on one dominant customer even before they are able to assess and evaluate the potential and adverse impact that can be caused by such a customer-product relationship. Thus in one sense, they become the appendage of the customer's business.

In any scenario if the dominant customer business faces a period of stress and adversity then the business which is depending on the customer suffer as a result. Its ability to mobilize orders from new customers and re-establish the brand in the market has been seriously impaired and this results in the business facing financial adversity. The business failed to foresee the potential risk in depending too much on a particular customer.

The Real challenge posed by the working of the ' Law of Substitution'!!

A large number of SMB entrepreneurs confine themselves to one sales avenue so long at the avenue is able to deliver the sales. No attention is paid to the potential risk if that particular sales avenue is suddenly disrupted by unavoidable and unforeseen external factors. In the able of an avenue B the sales figures of the business suddenly tumble and become the reason for financial distress. And they are invariably replaced by their competitor businesses in no time and this is the working of the law of substitution in the business world.

Growing the business in a holistic manner is the best survival technique that no business should lose sight of...businesses which have understood this rule have slowly found stability in consolidation and their survival in the growth initiatives. Business growth produced profitable business which could retain profit to meet the obligations to their stakeholders while being able to fund their growth objectives.

Having understood the necessity for setting a multi-pronged strategy of engaging different sales possibilities for growing sales, and depending on the type of business and the specific nature of products, or solutions or technologies dealt with by the company concerned, the sales department need to evaluate the different avenues and strategy approaches that could be suitable in the context of that particular business.

After making a choice of the specific sales strategy approach the Sales team formulates a sub goal and sales targets for each sales avenue the figures being compiled on the basis of data and information gathered from internal sales analysis data and market survey and research data .

From a Team resources perspective, within the sales team, roles and responsibilities are suitably assigned depending on the sales verticals and the sales strategy element and the sub goal fixed and thereby on the road to achieving the envisaged sales growth.

Businesses who have adopted strategy approach as above have benefited from higher sales year on year. These businesses have derived sales growth by addition or formulating and implementing strategies year after year and thus carving additional means of sales revenues.

Each such Revenue head or sales avenue newly created by engaging the strategy approach ,inherently possess the potential to grow and continuously scale up depending on the market trends and the intensity and focus of the teams efforts in terms of implementing the particular strategy and the agreed action plans.

This is the way of creating scalability in sales revenues and the road to actually create exponential or geometric progression both in terms of number of customer and sales values in a far lesser period of time.

## The imperative of holistic approach for the Business

The real question that the business faces : is the pre-sales side of the business growing too fast? that the back end is not able to handle? Are the front wheels of the car more smarter? when back wheel is not able to keep up?

In the evolution of businesses many founder entrepreneur play a key role in the marketing and sales thereby pivoting the revenue engine and leaving the other functions like operations, delivery, procurement, human resources department in the hands of his team members. In many of these organizations the sales side aggressively works for acquiring orders and in the process deploy a sizeable sales budget. While the business is able to create traction and a sizeable order pipeline the other functions of the business such as the operations department or the delivery department is unable to align with the business momentum created by sales department. In a sense this produces an imbalance in the form of the other departments being unable to perform their role of fulfilling the customer's orders. This situation is much like the car where the front tires are revolving at a high speed while the rear tires are unable to catch up with the rotation and thereby the car is unsteady and wobbling and likely to breakdown. to give more clarity to the above subject we may discuss the following question.

Is growth in sales and more sales and yet more sales the answer for businesses? what is the relevance of business consolidation?

When businesses reach the point that their products find a large enough market and there is a solid business traction and they have track record of several quarters of outstanding sales performance behind them with business and demand only growing and offering more and more growth and exponentially.

They come to the point where the flow of orders is far more than their capacity to handle and capacity to execute in time.

In other words if they were to accept the customer orders in the first place they may not be able to execute the order.

Businesses understand the reality that a steady phase of sales and business growth must be followed by an internal consolidation so that growth itself does not destabilize the business foundation and 'throw it off its feet'. Consolidation helps the business to gear up its capabilities streamline its processes and systems and mobilize financial and team resources for the level of preparedness to take on the benefit of the unfolding business opportunities in terms of Revenue and profitability and maintaining the financial stability.

Businesses who have not followed this vital principle about the intrinsic connection between growth and consolidation have landed themselves in deep crisis when the business has found itself unable to service even the orders that they have accepted from customers. In many cases this in turn produced adversity at their customer's end and with customers having initiated penal action, all this lead to total credibility loss and blemish on the brand image.

All eggs in one basket is a lot of risk - the challenge of just one sales avenue?

Generally, in SME businesses, when there is a discussion about Sales very often the discussion tends to be limited to Direct Sales. But with the passage of time invention of new technologies greater awareness and connectivity new avenues opened up for businesses to acquire clients. As the scenario got more complex with more product options, players , customers and market places businesses adopted strategic thinking by formulating strategies and processes in such a way that they may take maximum advantage of the emerging opportunities.

We have seen how, many successful businesses in diverse fields explore different sales avenues and strategies and thus produce scalability in revenues. We have seen that Direct sales is the sale methodology or a sales strategy which essentially entails client engagement happening through sales efforts of the internal Sales team in 'direct contact with the end client'.

In reality, many SME businesses struggle for years limiting themselves with 'selling opportunities' solely through their 'internal sales teams' which takes many months or even years to get a stable order stream, suffering severe cash deficits in the process.

Other avenues to generate sales by engaging with clients in other ways whether though a channel or dealers or online is given least seriousness. Invariably these potential lifelines for achieving sales growth are often ignored. Yet the point is that truly 'sales strategy' is not only about 'direct sales' there is a world of opportunity still beyond !

For instance in the case of a business with a distributed demand across the country it is necessary to address business opportunities to acquire customers in different geographies by appointment of dealers and distributors in each such selected locations or cities where there is potential.

Similarly, a large number of businesses have devised different approaches to acquire clients in multifarious ways and even engaged technologies to grow the Sales in a consistent and cost effective manner.

Through participation in Tender businesses have access to an additional channel for acquiring customers and leverage businesses. Here we are talking about Large corporates in the private sector as well as public or the government sectors engaging with vendors through the tender route having constituted portals for centralizing their purchases through tender.

Thus in order to ensure risk mitigation and scalability in sales businesses need to have a multipronged approach to sales and pursuing different sales avenues and strategies.

Growing Sales is not only about the sales department but more holistic?

As business organizations evolve, businesses and entrepreneurs realize the truth that producing sales is not only about optimizing their sales processes and optimum team performance at the sales department alone, but the play of many other facets of the business, in one sense a more holistic approach is needed to really ensure more customer acquisition and more sales growth.

Businesses who deal in products and solutions existing in a 'red ocean situation' with too many competitors realize this truth early enough. Notwithstanding their aggressive sales efforts, numbers of actual sales conversions constantly pose a challenge for the business given that the order books are not encouraging.

These business who possess minimum unique value propositions and differentiation who merely match their peer competitors in terms of product features, when faced with the 'price discerning customer' as the main segment in the 'red ocean -competitive market place' these businesses find it hard to sustain sales volumes.

Thus, everything being equal the business with the most 'Deep Pocket' or financial resources gain more in the aggressive market scenario either by offering longer credit or ridiculously low prices and so on. The subject business with no uniqueness to offer nor a financial capacity to match , simply fails in its attempt and has to give up.

Given that they have nothing to offer as a unique selling proposition and they are not able to talk about a functionally better product, or a product that has reinvented itself on the basis of state of the art hard ware and thereby reduced the bill of materials.

Similarly, they have not increased the functional capability by use of 'state of the art" components and to create and offer a better product at the same price that could claim to be a 'me better product'.

If they had done so , it certainly would be the offer that a well-informed customer would not simply refuse even in spite of some juicy financial offers by the other larger dominant player who has the same mundane product with a monetary package.

It is to be borne in mind that improved operational efficiencies, better bill of materials, functionally better products, products that align to the requirement of the customer, businesses that offer better post sales experience to customer, better return and refund policy and so on contribute directly to the capacity of the business to sell more. If these things are not addressed in time it may impair the sales person capacity to sell notwithstanding the sales budget and high competence of the sales personnel.

# CHAPTER SEVENTEEN

# Business Processes and Systems in Sales

**Sales strategy Implementation**

Business need to ensure that Strategies are translated in to action plans and the action plans are implemented without fail. It must be understood that every strategy formulated may lead to multiple action plans. For the success of the strategy implementation and for the outcome to flow to the business ,the action plan implementation is paramount. In this context let us seek answer to the question :

How is the Sales strategy implementation ensured through tracking of action plans?

Against each and every strategy formulated one or more action plan items are created for ensuring conversion of the strategies elements in to actual performance outcomes in terms of fulfilled goals and sub goals.

For implementing each action plan item specific responsibility and accountability is fixed on the team such as the sales manager or the specifically delegated members of the sales team. A time frame in terms of the date within which the action item needs to be duly implemented is also stipulated.

The next steps is to periodically review and track the progress made with respect to implementation of the strategy through the action items already decided and documented.

Strategy to action plan implementation tracker is the process by which the strategy and action plan linkages are documented systematically using software and systems and updated on a real time basis.

Through periodic weekly and fortnightly reviews effectively conducted within the sales department the timely completion of the action item is ensured.

In order to strengthen the performance management within the sales department Businesses need to Establish key performance indicators relevant to the sales discipline.

Through the process of sales review meetings the sales performance management need to be undertaken.

Sales/ marketing protocols ensure that reporting/ communication/ decision making/ leadership are managed effectively and help the department in the goal achievement.

**Relevance of Sales Review meetings**

In this way let us understand the relevance of sales review meeting protocol and documentation?

Business meeting protocols are defined to ensure that the sales review meetings are regularly conducted with defined agenda in a focussed manner and to ensure that the team is completely aligned to the goal.

In other words through the meetings which is convened at predetermined intervals, there is periodic review of the progress of action plans. This ensures planning and coordination within the team for achievement of the goal. Meetings are always conducted based on predetermined agenda and well defined meeting processes which ensure proper documentation.

To illustrate we can list the following twelve specific objectives of establishing meeting processes protocols and convening regular sales review meetings:

Focus on sales goals and complete alignment of the sales team in a common direction.

Regular assessment of milestones achieved vis a vis the goals and time frame setting helps build business momentum

Increase in Order closure possibilities ,by leveraging the team strength and wisdom.

Communication gaps are ironed out to prevent conflicts, through timely coordinated actions.

Management has an accurate insight with regard to the actual differences within the team which cause potential conflict.

Teams become very cohesive and pursue a unified direction.

Identification of weak and missing links within the sales team become possible to take corrective action in a timely manner.

Process gaps become clear and helps the team to formulate necessary processes within the department..

Systems and automation needs within the sales department become clear and there is a unified consensus on the nature of system to be installed.

Cross selling opportunities within the client business become visible and leads to higher sales.

Interdepartmental coordination vis a vis the other department like Operations, Delivery, Finance is thereby improved.

Problem zones and disaster possibilities show up much earlier to adopt preventive steps.

**Installing Processes**

Let us understand why is it important to install processes in the marketing & Sales department?

Establishing processes in the marketing and sales department is the key to ensure that the sales goals are achieved through the implementation of the strategies and action plans. All the processes which are part of the marketing and sales department are collectively called customer acquisition process. These processes collectively enable the sales Team to function as one block and they are completely aligned with the Goals. The processes also facilitate the team members to fully leverage the synergies from their collective and cohesive team work to jointly achieve the goal.

Pre-sales processes constitute an important part of the customer acquisition processes.

In summary, all the processes that manage the activities at the Presales stage which essentially cover each and every single milestone being part and parcel of the pre-sales engine of the business.

The distinct stages in the pre-sales area can be broadly illustrated as under:

Generation of leads or prospects

Qualifying or validation of the leads or prospects

Engagement with the prospect through visit, call or correspondence.

Submission of quotation or offers to the target client

Negotiation for finalization either through visit, call or meeting.

Obtaining the documented order with the terms and conditions.

Ideally business processes ensure that the information and document flow from the stage to stage is tracked so that no prospect is missed out and prospect which can potentially be converted into an order are diligently tracked in order to ensure definitive order closure.

While most SMB Businesses and their sales departments do not always miss an order to close sales with a particular customer on any count, on the contrary they could lose an order owing to a small inadvertent error which was caused on account of lack of pre sales processes.

The second process that is relevant in the context of the Customer retention process which is essentially all the sub processes that all together fulfil the customer retention strategies that are painstakingly formulated by businesses from time to time. In the customer retention processes the marketing and sales function plays the pivotal role but the operations and delivery department also play an important role in producing a higher customer retention rate.

## Systems and Automation

After understanding Sales processes let us study the relevance of installing systems and Automation and how do they contribute to Sales Goals?

For the smooth and effective functioning of the business acquisition processes it is necessary to install systems and automation in the sales and marketing team through installation of appropriate IT tools, systems etc. and thereby create standardization of records, forms and information while ensuring accuracy of the information. There are software applications marketed by reputed companies who offer CRM software solutions to specifically manage the resales stage effectively .These system and automaton options can be can be evaluated by SMB businesses and then implemented within their businesses.

Automation obscures the need for human resources intervention and thereby because instrumental in reducing the workforce in the sales department. On the other hand the systems provide the information processing backbone and analytical data for effective management of the sales department .

For Repetitive tasks which require data accuracy, high degree of standardization, limited discretion this becomes a great advantage as the system is able to generate huge output in a matter of time with utmost accuracy and least supervision.

Larger number of SMB business lack a complete perspective with regard to the importance and the imperatives for identifying the systems and automation requirements of the sales department and the business as a whole and the need for making an appropriate capex plan for implementation of the same.

Systems and automation are extremely important for the success of a business enterprise and meeting the sales objectives. Systems and automation are as important as the machinery, equipment, other infrastructure for the success of a business enterprise. Businesses have to understand their requirements from the systems and automation and then set the objectless for making the choice of the solutions and technologies clearly.

They need to define data processing needs accurately, the reporting requirements, the information analysis and feedback, the checks and balance to control resources before making a choice of the right system which will meet the business objectives.

In most SMB enterprises decisions with regard to system and automation is taken based on budget centric approach rather than impact centric or objectivity approach which maps the system specification of the proposed system with the actual requirement.

Hence, decisions taken do not have a holistic perspective, and the system or automation solution chosen for implementation on the idea of budget limits invariably end up being unable to meet the objectives of the business. Invariably these type of Capex decisions end up as losses as they produce no tangible benefit at the same time take a lot of the management time and energy before being shelved.

Ideally, decisions regarding systems and automation as aforementioned need to be taken after extensive study of the business, strategic and financial information requirements and based on merit of the solution that is being chosen. It is better to avoid a halfhearted decision based on a budgetary limitation and overlooking the fact that the system or automation will not completely meet the requirements.

...where the investment proposal is correlated to the potential contribution to sales growth in terms of volumes and numbers or value, improved business and financial decisions, avoidance of losses, better people accountability, checks and balances and greater internal control the decision is more likely to meet the business growth and profitability objectives.

## Marketing and Sales Budgets

We need to extend our discussion regarding marketing and sales processes in order to cover Sales and Marketing Budgets.

It needs to be borne in mind that the effectiveness of the marketing and sales department and the outcomes that are ultimately produced will depend on the team resources and other material resources that are deployed and the availability of the financial budgets at the right time for the purpose of actual implementation of the sales strategies through action plans.

Effective budgeting as part of the financial planning will depend on forecasting, accurate resource estimation. In other words accurate estimation of the material and people resources required for marketing and customer acquisition. When based on the strategy choice, forecasting and market research the budget is carefully allocated considering the target customer niche and their purchasing behavior it is more likely to lead to optimal and viable levels of customer acquisition cost and ultimately produce tangible sales revenue.

On the other hand, when businesses spend marketing budgets without a clear understanding of their target customers and their purchasing habits, it can result in a "cash burn" with little or no potential for generating revenue. It is important for businesses to carefully consider their marketing strategies and allocate budgets accordingly in order to achieve the best return on investment.

## Sales Documentation

What is Sales Documentation ?what is the importance of Documentation in Sales?

Sales documentation is a critical part of the sales process as it provides a record of the interactions and activities from the identification of a prospect to the point of obtaining a customer order. This documentation is important for ensuring that the sales team is aligned and coordinated in order closure and post-sales marketing efforts, as well as in providing necessary support for order fulfillment. In this way, sales documentation helps to ensure smooth and successful implementation of the sales process and a transparent work flow within the sales department.

## Sales Collaterals

What is the importance of Sales Collaterals?

Successful businesses and their marketing and sales departments exercise great care with regard to preparation of the sales Briefcase consisting of the sales collaterals, samples, brochures in such a way that if the sales personnel meets the decision maker at the customer's end the possibility of order closure is not hindered for want of any of information .

## Standardization of sales offers

What is the importance of standardization of sales quotation or offers?

After identification of the sales prospect and eliciting the customer's need for the specific product or the solution the next task of the sales department is to submit the quotation or the offer to the customer and close the order.

The biggest challenge faced by the small and medium SME entrepreneur is that from the time of identifying a customer prospect and qualifying the customer, proposal or quotation takes longer time for preparation and submission to the customer concerned.

Such delays in submission of formal quotation or offers to customers happens even when the business has received a highly potential sales enquiry for the products manufactured by the business which in turn has a high likelihood of conversion in to a sale order. If the customer concerned is in a hurry to finalize the order then a late response or quotation not submitted in time can invariably become the reason for the business to lose the order.

A quotation which is Delayed in terms of submission to the target client reflects badly on the business concerned. This leads to erosion of customer confidence on the quality delivery and generally the perception about the business in general.

One of the paramount and identified reason for delay in submission of quotation is lack of standardization in preparing proposals and quotation to customers. Even though the requirement from the customer are within the standard product range or the range of solutions the business has not evolved a proper structure or common standard of contents and information covering the repetitive matters and some aspects like pricing policy and credit policy and other terms are not available in a standardized manner. Let us look at the anomalies caused on account of non-standardization of the quotation:

Proposal format and structure being not standardized, results in slower response to customers.

Content of document being part of the quotation not updated delays proposal submission.

Revisions and improvisations from proposal to proposal not captured.

Standard clauses which are permanent not preprinted leading to unwarranted repetitive work.

Brochure content and web site content is not exactly matching...sets wrong impression in the customers mind.

Correspondence contents have several irrelevant information remain unedited, and slowly the customer starts ignoring the correspondence totally.

Among SMB businesses, in a particular market more efficient peer business even though possess lower technical competence, lower quality of solution invariably succeeds in getting the order from the customer. The SMB business with higher technical capability and better solution loses the potential offer. The peer competitor had even though possessed technical and other limitations had standardized their offer submission and internal sales processes to ensure speedy response as expected by the customer and succeeded in closing the order.

In short, the SMB business was ready to encash the business opportunity to close their sale and on the strength of their readiness and response they obtained the order from the customer and thereby substituted the more technically competent competitor business which had higher technical merit but a badly organized business environment.

Preparation and submission of quotations or offers to the customer well in time is as important as the sales activity covering identifying customer prospects and providing demo for the products in other words the entire field activity.

Improper team and resource management within the sales team also become a cause for delay in submission of quotation to clients. On the one hand SMB businesses have limited financial resource ability and hence have fewer people in the team with most resources multitasking and engaged in front line sales activity along with the back end coordination. In such cases processes, systems, automation, standardization of tasks and information which are repetitive become paramount for speedy response system with respect to client engagement.

**Is the Business ' Deal Ready'**

A pertinent question that needs to be addressed to an SMB is whether the business is deal ready? in other words the readiness of the business in terms of capacity to close the order?

Large number of SMB businesses essentially face the problem described as 'No deal readiness' ...The irony is that after intense marketing and selling efforts if a customer actually appears at the door step of the Business the entrepreneur realizes that the sales department of that business is not able to close the sales order as there is lack of readiness within the sales department or the business at large .The reasons for the business could be diverse which essentially form the missing links. This could for example be lack of sufficient information, or documentation or delay in quotation or exact pricing issues or lack of the right type of sales resources with skill to close the order, so on and so forth.

Most Businesses ultimately blame customers and the market or any other extraneous factor as the cause for their negative fortunes? rather than themselves ?

But the fact remains that entrepreneurs who built strong businesses after understanding the cardinal truth that a business has to be prepared and geared sufficiently in order to be able to identify, source and closes orders from customers while building and maintaining internal sales processes backed by a trained competent team that ensure continuity and consistency of performance period after period.

**Communication in the area of sales**

Let us now understand the importance and role of communication in the area of sales?

Communication is the single most important function within and outside of a business, it is equally important for all the facets of the business. In this section we are referring to the specific role and importance of communication in the marketing and sales department of the business which has huge ramification on the outcomes of the sales initiatives and the business success at large.

Successful businesses which have a robust sales engine invariably ensure internal processes and well framed policies to manage the entire gamut of communication in the sales department which essentially each and every form of communication that emerge out of the engagement of the business with the external fraternity starting with customers ,dealers channel partners and so on.

On the contrary, in the case of a large number of SMB businesses communication is not given the required importance and emphasis and the entrepreneur do not understand the ramification caused by weaknesses and aberrations in the communication system on the ultimate sales outcomes .In other words there is a complete lack of understanding on the importance of communication in the area of sales.

For ready reference, a large number of SMB business do not have clear cut well specified and documented guidelines and policies with regard to communication in terms of the following:

(a) Content of communication -general and specific communication

(b) Authorized person who is vested with power to communicate

(c)People within the team to be copied on a particular written communication

(d) when to escalate the communication to the superior or senior

(e) how to handle complaints and angry communication from Customers

(f) how to handle after sales and service calls and so on.

The entire communication engine is extremely shaky which has adverse impacts on the performance of the sales team and the acquisition of new orders, increase in customers, customer retention, team work within the sales team and lastly on the achievement of the sales plan all of which can prove financially very costly for the business.

As illustration of the aforementioned aspects in the context of large number of SMB businesses who have a serious lack of policies and processes with respect to communication we are placing below four directly relatable impacts:

a)Word of mouth has low shelf life...Written correspondence provides track to defend against blames from customers.

b) Customer related information can be inadvertently forgotten or missed..

c) Customer feedback is susceptible to even misrepresentation within the organization.

d) Internal conflicts between the Sales staff and Interdepartmental conflicts between Sales and Operations get carried to Customers...this can causes negative perception.

Similarly, lack of alignment and mismatches in the communication within the sales department of SMB businesses become reason to cause negative perception in the mind of the customer and even result in loss of sales prospects and customers.

1)Content of Correspondence does not match with content in other sales materials.

2) Between Brochures and Marketing material there are mismatches with regard to information-version changes.

3)Contents in the web site is not updated well in time and there are mismatches with other sales collaterals and the sales communication.

SMB businesses need to ensure formulation of communication policies and processes which are adhered to by the sales department to ensure growth in sales, retention of customers, growth in new customers and internal coordination and teamwork within the sales department and the ensure sound inter department viz sales and operations coordination and effective team work.

# CHAPTER EIGHTEEN

# MAKING A ROBUST, COMMITTED SALES TEAM

What is the importance of the sales team up-skilling? What are the ways in which an SMB business achieve the objective?

Up skilling the sales and marketing persons with sales skills ,specific product knowledge, dealing with knowledge management, new trends in the field of sales, and generally improving the team's communication ability produce a high performing sales team. The sales performance is more likely to positively impact in terms of more customer order conversions from the prospect stage to order closure. Opportunity to learn is an important value that make employee want to work with an employer.

Large number of forward looking organizations set sales team training objectives which cover the sales team upskilling and training protocols and policies.

To ensure implementation of these objectives internal training processes are created within the sales department in conjunction with the HR department. The actual training is carried out by the senior sales supervisor and seniors who possess understanding of the sales domain along with the HR resource. In other larger SMB organizations, the periodic sales training is conducted by the senior sales personnel and partly through external sales training experts who ensures upgradation of the skills of the sales personnel on a continuous, systematic and periodic basis. Through a review process the impact of the up skilling and the knowledge upgradation on the sales persons sales performance is tracked.

The HR department in conjunction with the Sales head will rely on the performance appraisal system to measure the actual performance improvement of the sales resource in achieving the targets and thereby rate the effectiveness of the training program.

**Importance of Fixation of sales incentive for sales personnel in SME Businesses**

Fixation of sales incentive is a function that require close coordination between the sales and the Finance department of a business in conjunction with the corporate or the top management.

In SMB businesses this subject is not provided the right focus and decisions are invariably taken in an arbitrary manner without any clear principles and formulating a documented policy. Sales incentives could become the single biggest cause for attrition of the sales staff and most often the most performing sales person.

Number of businesses who have moved in to the sales incentive system after a few years of not having a system of paying incentives that too without a conscious plan and an in-depth understanding of the subject have landed up with discontented employee who felt they are not recognized and therefore quit the employment !!

As aforementioned, in SMB Businesses sales incentive policy is arbitrarily announced without a detailed holistic study of all the relevant aspects, the scenario in peer organization from the same industry, the percentages and the system adopted by them, the long term financial viability, the upsides and the downsides of implementing the system etc.

In some SMB organizations without pre assessing the monetary impact...a certain percentage of sales is arbitrarily promised as sales incentives. In actual calculation the end figures sometimes become unrealistic and unaffordable with a virtual possibility of causing aberration within the system. Similarly in the case of businesses which offer goods on credit the sales incentive payment is made only against actual sales were the business has collected the payment after the credit period.

In the case of SMB business once the aberration or the technical unviability is understood the decision to pay incentive is summary reversed by the management which in turn causes a blemish on the business as a whole which could make potential and high performing sales personnel to have a reason to leave the employment.

It is hence extremely essential that before taking a decision to introduce a sales incentive system within a business a comprehensive study is conducted across(a) similar businesses in the same sector and related sector(b)understanding the incentive payment structure (c) rates applied and terms and conditions(d) actual incentive disbursement payment conditions and forfeiture of sales incentives in specific cases(e) period of service to become eligible (e) total limit of incentive payment. Based on the above aspects a comprehensive policy needs to be created covering all the aspects for standardization and uniform implementation.

**How to constitute a balanced sales team in an SMB scenario?**

Having understood the meaning of the word direct sales in the business context let us examine how SME business manage direct sales goals to achieve their business goals.

From time immemorial we have seen that businesses primarily create a sales team consisting of a few people and hit the road on day one with or without adequate planning.

The sales persons may or may not be formally trained in the products to the desired level, the sales person's may or may not possess the required sales mindset and skill to prospect sales leads and close the orders.

On the one hand, these businesses invariably incur the cost of hiring of sales resources and the sales related expenses month after month.

On the other hand, in a matter of few months they realize that they are not able to secure sufficient orders, or generate sufficient sales leads, thereby result in operations department becoming idle causing losses and negative cash flows. These businesses wake up to the actual realty that the sales team is not performing.

In these situations the possibility is that the sales person is likely to blame the company for his nonperformance citing one or other reason which could be quality issues, high price, untimely delivery, poor after sales, improper complaint handling etc.

In organizations that are less organized and having insufficient sales processes, documented salesperson wise performance data, the sales person is less likely to recognize or admit the deficiencies on his part be it sales skills or lack of proper efforts, or non-adherence to the defined sales policies and available sales processes etc. When businesses see their sales goal achievement to be attained by depending solely on the frontline sales personnel .... there is a chance that they would be proved wrong.

To accomplish sales, the sales personnel who are part of the sales department handling front line sales require selling skill, and the sales department as a whole require to function as an integrated team with clear roles and responsibilities as between team members , ensure adherence to sales processes, while engaging necessary automaton, software systems for data standardization and accuracy .

In other words, more organized SMB businesses clearly understand that Direct Sales is a game to be played by creating a balanced and complete sales team with skilled members who handle the multiple roles and responsibilities which when collectively synergized produce the sales goals. And this rule will hold good for all alike be it a small SMB Business or a Large business entity.

With this clarity we need to look at the subject of how to constitute a sales team for handling the direct sales business opportunity with a direct connect to the customer and the market place along with the need for appointing and managing a channel or dealer network, handling the online sales activity besides opportunities for sales through Tender.

An ideal sales engine for a SMB business which is in a growth stage can be illustrated as follows:

a)Front line sales person who will handle customer prospecting , customer lead generation and field sales activities.

b)Sales supervisor in the nature of a manager who will handle planning, coordination and control of the sales team.

c)A Sales coordinator inducted at the back end who handles client or customer correspondence, Quotation or proposal submission, order follow-up, and after sales collection of receivables, if the sale is on credit basis.

In the case of micro businesses who cannot afford a 3 people team as illustrated above the point to be noted is that there are three different distinct roles which has to be necessarily handled and the three aforementioned roles require slightly different skill sets, experience, job knowledge etc.

In the case of smaller organizations one or more of these roles are invariably handled by the founder entrepreneurs themselves, while the others are handled by the team member.But the core is to understand the synergistic purpose of creating a comprehensive and balanced team in the above manner to leverage and optimize sales performance month on month in a consistent manner and registering envisaged growth as well.

Successful SMB's understand the principle and constitute their sales team in conformity with a well thought organization chart with team members consisting of resources who handle the field sales lead and prospecting position/ resource handling back end client coordination / third resource as team lead who helps in order closure and the team coordination and the internal inter department coordination.

**Importance of sales team retention processes in SMB businesses?**

Retaining sales persons on the job for a reasonable period of time ensuring that they do not leave the job on account of frivolous reasons prematurely is a challenge that many SMB businesses face. Invariably the flight of sales personnel from the organization is invariably to join larger organization who offer and pay better salaries and overall provide better working atmosphere and more attractive compensation packages with additional perquisites.

In a competitive world it is extremely essential for the sales department to act in conjunction with the HR department and frame a comprehensive sales resources retention strategy and implement processes that will ensure the implementation of the same.

A Large number of SMB businesses have managed to have a low attrition track record with minimum employee desertion and loss of competent resources to the competitor.

They have managed the situation by implementing an effective sales team retention strategy which essentially track the following :

Skill versus job profile in other words right job for the right person, good teamwork and balance within the sales team with common direction, sales team real-time performance management processes using the right systems ,software and automation, performance appraisal versus right communication to employee, Well-structured Organization Chart and properly defined roles and responsibilities, Employee recognition through reward and recognition systems, Fair salary packages and properly structured sales incentive systems, recognizing negative employees early enough and detoxifying the bad influences, ushering in a very balanced employee culture with high employer esteem in the mind of the employee, putting in place Structured hiring and severance policies

Review of Feedback from exit interviews and so on.

Let us look at the adverse impact of Lack of travel allowance policies

Let us understand the adverse impacts of lack of clear processes and policies covering travel allowances and related issues relating to Sales Persons can cause disillusionment and hinder their satisfaction and motivation. Ensuring that salespeople are able to travel and move freight smoothly and without issues is important for maintaining their engagement and motivation. Adopting clear policies and procedures for managing salesperson travel and related concerns can help to prevent disruptions and keep the sales team focused on their goals. It is important for businesses to prioritize the well-being and support of their salespeople in order to foster a positive and productive work environment.

# CHAPTER NINETEEN

# EMERGENCE OF THE DIGITAL REVOLUTION - ONLINE STRATEGIES

Emergence of the digital revolution during the last decade has in-fact created huge business opportunities for all business and particularly SMB business without bounds.

It is true that in the short term this has disrupted the marketplace and threatened the very existence of many SMB organizations who had not foreseen the potential impact of changes brought by the new online business paradigm on their businesses. This has caused many businesses to even wind up their shops and establishments pushing them into oblivion.

Other more visionary businesses and entrepreneurs foresaw the transformation and the digital revolution early enough and therefore prepared their businesses and themselves to deal with the new imminent change and the challenges and opportunities that accompanied the tech evolution. They initiated and ushered in holistic business transformation within their businesses thereby reinventing their organization to face the new emerging world and the new rules of business.

These businesses approached the challenge as the new opportunity for their business to survive and grow in a manner hitherto unprecedented that too with far lesser bounds. For instance they could foresee the huge opportunity that is available to their businesses to achieve customer growth at exponential rate, given that physical or geographical boundaries was no longer relevant and in essence did not exist anymore. In other words this opened the possibility of acquiring customers in new untapped geographic regions which otherwise they could not have addressed in the conventional offline business model.

**New paradigms and realities to address Online Sales Opportunities**

Let us look at some of the new paradigms and realities ushered in for businesses in order to address Online business opportunities ?

In the online business world, the new rules for conducting business require businesses to be more organized, process-oriented, and automated, as well as more responsive to opportunities and customer needs. The time frame for responding to business opportunities and providing quotes to prospects is often limited, and businesses must be ready to provide comparative pricing information in real-time. Proposal and quotation submission must be standardized and done quickly.

Customer feedback is also critical in the online business world, and negative feedback about a business's product quality can quickly lead to the loss of future customers. To succeed online, businesses must have a holistic approach to handling customer orders, including packing, shipping, and delivery, as well as handling returns and refunds. They must also have effective strategies for managing the "last mile" of delivery, including working with couriers and logistics vendors to ensure high standards of quality and customer service.

At the most basic level we are looking at the key issues that become relevant as follows:

At the basic level Sellers and buyers perspectives in the new world had to completely change. Online business-related technologies and solutions offered cost effective purchasing avenues to customers. Businesses could become Geography agnostic both in the matter of acquiring and transacting sales with customers and for others to meet their raw material procurement objectives. Buyers have more product options and choices with better visibility and better price comparison and leverage. Offering schemes, discount offers to customers for Dealing with stock liquidation, clearance of inventory carry over became just a click away. Online Sale opportunities for businesses through marketplaces like Amazon provided huge opportunity for scalability. Businesses were no longer limited by their pre-sales resources team to acquire leads as they could source potential customer leads through portals through B2B Channels.

Businesses created a sales avenue of selling directly to customer by setting up their own e commerce site dealing with their products and services and creating back end for accomplishing the same. Online business primarily obviated the need for meeting between seller and buyer in order to facilitate the sales / purchase transaction.

For taking the decision to buy, increasingly customers relied on the information presented by the Seller on the web site and regarding (a) product (b) their capacity to deliver (c) testimonials or ratings of earlier customers besides information regarding the organization that is available in the public domain. And in doing so, customers take critical decisions regarding Price, credit terms, Advance Payment terms, delivery dates without the seller and the buyer ever meeting in person.

The most age old limitation faced by the SME customer in terms of being confined to identifying customers within their immediate and proximate geographies given their limited capital and sales budget became the subject of the past .

In the digital world, there were virtually no geographical boundaries to acquiring customers and transacting business. The only relevant factor that remained to be addressed was whether the business had the capacity to deliver the product or services to the customer.

In the digital era, technology enabled more interactive engagement between the customer and the brand. This caused businesses to have an opportunity to move closer to the customer, gauge and survey the customer behavior, understanding the customer choices, the customer pain points and problems and so on.

This deep customer insight helped brands to design an appropriate product that is most likely to be completely aligned to meet the customer need thereby addressing his specific pinpoints while meeting the customers value criteria in terms of budget and the financial objectives.

Increasing choices available to customers with no limitation to access supply and more connected market places provide level playing field.

Customers having multiple choices available to them it was no longer possible to deal with retaining customers without having concrete customer retention strategies. Businesses competed with one another in the process of drawing the customer's attention with the objective of increasing their respective market share. Owing to a more digitally connected world which provided level playing field for all businesses, organization's that were smaller no longer faced the limitation of size and scale of the Business while establishing a presence in the market.

In the digital age, customer focus is key to business success. This means aligning products or services to comprehensively meet the needs and requirements of customers in terms of functionality, value, and timely delivery. By understanding and fully meeting the expectations of customers, businesses can grow by adding new customers, retaining existing ones, and increasing sales revenue per customer through the continuous addition of new products.

To support this growth, businesses must adopt cutting-edge technology and automation within their operations, delivery, inventory, and even at the sales end. In the past, investment in technology was seen as a cost rather than an opportunity, but in the new business environment, both operational and capital expenditures on technology are considered opportunities.

Startup enterprises that identify a significant problem faced by customers and create innovative, disruptive solutions using cutting-edge technologies that fully align with customer requirements can often raise sufficient funding from angel investors and venture capital funds to pursue their vision.

In a more connected, digitally-enabled marketplace with numerous options available to customers, it is essential for businesses to have concrete customer retention strategies to compete for market share. Smaller businesses no longer face the limitations of size and scale in establishing a presence in the market.

Is the new Buyer perspectives on Online sourcing the new business opportunity?

Business-to-business (B2B) portals have provided a solution to the challenge of efficiently procuring raw materials, components, and other inputs for businesses. These portals bring buyers and sellers together quickly, allowing businesses to save time and financial resources that would otherwise be spent on vendor development.

Traditionally, the procurement process has been a source of pain for businesses, particularly manufacturing firms that need to source a large number of components and parts. Online B2B portals have revolutionized this process by creating an online platform for buyers and vendors to register, transact, and conclude business deals. By using B2B portals, businesses can optimize the cost of procurement, including the salaries and administrative costs of the procurement team.

Let us turn our attention to Changes in Perspective of those businesses being Vendors who are the sellers in the B2B platforms?

Businesses that engage in online sales and serve as vendors on B2B platforms no longer need an internal pre-sales team to prospect for sales enquiries and orders using traditional offline sales approaches. Instead, these businesses can access leads or enquiries posted by customers looking to procure goods through the B2B platform.

As a result of this shift, these organizations must focus on strengthening their business proposal teams, including standardizing proposals and quotations, implementing new systems and automation, and improving technical and cost estimation processes. The lead prospecting team within the sales department becomes less important, while the proposal team becomes more vital.

# CHAPTER TWENTY

# Internal Business Realignment

In this section let us discuss the imperatives for businesses in the form of internal Business Realignment to address Online business opportunities?

Accessing international business and global customers becomes a reality.

Thus, these businesses which adapted their business to address the online business found that that their products were becoming increasingly visible to international customers and opening business potential from global markets. This provided a larger business canvas to source international business and achieve scalability .Having found the right access to international customers the job that the SME businesses had to do was to upgrade their products and services in terms of quality, quantity ,delivery and service efficiency besides international certifications and so on.

**Change in the marketing and sales approaches**

Thus the approach and criteria of the new online customer prospect while taking a buying decision depended on ratings of old customers, even the actual number of past customers who have posted testimonials regarding the reliability of the services. Of course the core factors driving customer decision remain products quality, product packing, durability, no of days for delivery of the product, pricing and discounts offered , so on and so forth.

Online business took the advantage of secondary and primary market surveys that used technology extensively to extract collate and analyze customer data and feedback and record preferences, assess customer behavior across different profiles all of which being pure data thereby consolidated as market intelligence that provided key inputs for decision making to the sales and marketing departments and responding with focused 'go to market' strategies.

It is clear that there are huge changes in marketing sales approaches in the online business model. For instance in the conventional sales approach where sales is accomplished by the direct sales team the sales acumen of the concerned sales resource thereby influenced the order closure. Similarly if we take the conventional channel sales approach involving distributors and stores the sales promoters and theses persons play an important role in the deal closure.

Thus, it may be said that in the online business model for many businesses the customer is able to access the product directly through a process of disintermediation where the erstwhile role of the conventional sales person or the pre sales engine has been largely substituted.

Real time updating of the website, blogs and the information on social media, Payment gateways by installing processes in the pre-sales department is extremely critical.

The business digital and information framework need to be supported by appropriate software systems ERP automation, innovative technologies like robotics and AI,

To ensure brand credibility there is need for high transparency, standardization of the offerings and the collaterals, attractive product brochures, further price policies, including discounts, schemes need to be clearly laid down.

In order to succeed in the online business world, it is critical for businesses to keep their website, blogs, and social media channels updated in real-time, as well as to have effective payment gateways in place. To support their digital and information framework, businesses should consider implementing software systems like ERP automation and innovative technologies like robotics and AI. Ensuring brand credibility is also important, and this can be achieved through transparency, standardization of offerings and collateral materials, and clear communication of pricing policies, including discounts and schemes. Attractive product brochures can also help to enhance brand credibility and appeal to potential customers.

## Role of influencers

In the digitally enabled market place the role of independent influencers accentuated over the years with reputed Influencers with track record and large following therefore played a major role in influencing the buying decisions of customers and providing a deal of exponentially to the particular brand. Thus Businesses engaged the services of professional influencers to play the role in sales augmentation and higher customer acquisition and growth in new customers and so on.

'No safe havens' in the market place for brands and channels

Increasingly, businesses realized that online business opportunities disrupted the conventional 'safe exclusive geographies' that was available to brands with no peer competitor to challenge or any other threat to losing their traditional market share. This scenario caught number of brands by surprise which drove them to the brink of loss of sales, customer ,market share and so on.

Businesses that are customer focused have more possibility to succeed.

In the era of the tech based digital revolution that identified new ethos for managing businesses, like never before, customers and their needs increasingly became the central focus.

Thus, a high degree of focus on customer centricity placed the paramount need for aligning the product or service to comprehensively fit the customer's needs and requirements in terms of functionality, value and timely delivery.

In doing so, the rules and ideas regarding investment and financial exposure with regarding to owing and funding operational assets underwent major redefinition.

With the understanding of the customer expectation through total alignment with the customer it was possible for businesses to see clearly the way to grow their business by adding customers, retaining existing customers, and increasing sales revenue values per customer by continuously adding new products thereby forming a comprehensive product mix around the customer needs.

To deal with the business growth momentum, internally there was need for businesses to adopt cutting edge technology and automation within the operations, delivery ,inventory, and even at the sales end.

Thus, unlike in the past when businesses virtually resented investment in the new technologies and technology based Capex, in the new business order investment in technology both OPEX and CAPEX was considered as an opportunity instead of considering the same as merely another Cost head.

Many businesses that were structured as 'STARTUP enterprises' which identified a large enough problem faced by the customer created an 'innovative and disruptive' 'never thought before' and 'novel technology solution using cutting edge technologies that complexly aligned with the customers requirement. These startup's managed to raise sufficient funding from Angel funding and venture capital funds to pursue their business Vision.

**New Financial dynamics**

How Price as a factor became even more critical?

Changing in internal cost alignments and changing revenue to cost proportions

Changes in business model produced new cost alignments .These alignments obviated many cost heads while adding other cost heads.

In the overall analysis, businesses could become leaner and meaner and run the business with far lower working capital availability.

Businesses dared to become 'operational asset light' while engaging industry collaborations to work with vendors and job workers to support with components and intermediate products and so on for aligning with the new operating and delivery model. This also resulted in changing revenue to cost proportions .

Many businesses in trading and manufacturing moved their business to the Online space and they were no longer burdened with many cost items particularly establishment cost which was high under the old business model.

Increased pressure on costing and efficiencies and lower cost for the same functionality.

These Businesses that moved to the Online business space faced increased pressure on their bottom lines and profitability. There was increased pressure on businesses to manage their cost and optimize internal resource utilization efficiency .

They were devoid of a robust response system which can ensure speedy response to potential enquiries from prospective customers. This in turn caused them to lose out to competitors who were faster in their response to potential business opportunities which caused financial stress.

Online procurement opportunities provided tremendous potential for businesses to source from across the globe and thereby benefit from currency arbitrage and take advantage of regional price advantages with real time availability of cost information inputs for expedient pricing decisions, this helped business cost competitive and maintain profitability.

**Pricing challenges, total price transparency and freer availability**

These factors increased the pressure on businesses to deal with their pricing decisions and formulate their pricing policies to deal with market changes in a fast and expeditious manner .As there is greater price transparency across the online market place, potential customers could make well informed decisions with reliable price comparisons being available to them.

**Higher Price for novelty, innovation, new product releases**

In the online space, customers harbored continuous aspiration for novelty. Thus, businesses were under pressure to create new product versions, more frequently. In order to focus on new product innovation, businesses were required to become asset lite and strong with their innovation and continuous technology development initiatives. Supply chain optimization and greater degree of cooperation among the manufacturers within the component manufacturing clusters made enormous business sense in terms of providing economies of scale.

Extensive use of cutting-edge technologies helped businesses to optimize resources, limit their investment in inventory, adopting 'just in time inventory 'based production models and totally obviating obsolete and slow moving inventory and optimizing product contribution and higher profitability.

**Holistic approach through Business Realignment to address Online business opportunities**

Business Realignment preparing the business to address online opportunities called for a complete business realignment which had to start at the core strategic business level. There was need for a complete bottoms up redefinition of the departments of marketing/ sales/ delivery/ payment/ after sales services and so on. And simultaneously businesses had to reinvent their businesses internally formulating the right strategies and action plans to achieve them, installing processes and policies, technologies, systems and automation to build a solid framework to address this emerging opportunity.

Business Realignment Complete Optimization of the delivery engine in terms of : digitalization of information and records including product information- catalogues to ensure retrievability , followed by standardization of pricing policies including schemes and discounts, high response speed to Customer calls, robust order handling system, which ensures monitoring and timely product delivery, adherence to Product quality and specification standards, clear terms for rejection and returns, product replacements, customer redressal , post product sales installation support. Online promotions and marketing initiatives have a huge impact and can trigger business opportunities. Branding: Online businesses have a huge leverage through proper branding and communication. People Skill Upgrading the existing team members with skill sets and competencies to handle the new challenges and business opportunities provided by the online business.

**Online Sales strategies and new Business Model to address Online Business opportunities**

Let us the subject of 'Business Model' in the online Business context?

Thus, in order to deal with the online business opportunities unfolding through the digital evolution businesses had to increasingly engage 'digital transformation technologies' to acquire customers with the conventional 'business model' of the organization having undergone complete transformation. Business models such as B2C,D2C, B2B and many different derivatives of the above came in vogue with different entrepreneurs adopting approaches that addressed their need for Revenue scalability. Businesses in the product space and the services space adopted approaches that best suited the needs of customer acquisition, revenue scalability. Thus online businesses rewrote all the hitherto rules that dictated businesses existing in the conventional offline models where physicality, size of offices, sales team member size and so on became important considerations for business acquisitions.

Let us discuss the online strategies that can be formulated by a small SME business in its initial formative period.

In a nutshell, for leveraging online business opportunities, businesses can focus on several key strategies, including building a digital footprint for their business through records and information, optimizing their website to convert visitors into potential customers, and leveraging social media to understand customer behavior. Blog creation, email campaigns, and digital marketing campaigns through paid ads on social media can also be effective in increasing customer attention and engagement. Engaging influencers can also help to create traction for the brand and drive business outcomes. let us discuss each of the above strategies in detail:

Create a website: A website is a key tool for building your online presence and reaching potential customers. Make sure to design a website that is visually appealing, easy to navigate, and mobile-friendly. Use social media: Social media can be a powerful tool for reaching potential customers and building your brand. Choose the platforms that make the most sense for your business and create a consistent presence on those platforms.

Email marketing: Email marketing can be an effective way to reach potential customers and stay top-of-mind with existing ones. Make sure to create an email list and send regular newsletters or promotional emails to your subscribers. Search engine optimization (SEO):

SEO involves optimizing your website and online content to rank highly in search engine results. This can help drive traffic to your website and improve your online visibility.

Pay-per-click (PPC) advertising: PPC advertising involves placing ads on search engine results pages or other websites and paying a fee each time someone clicks on your ad. This can be an effective way to reach potential customers and drive traffic to your website.

Influencer marketing: Influencer marketing involves partnering with influencers on social media or other platforms to promote your products or services to their followers. This can be an effective way to reach a new audience and build brand awareness.

Content marketing: Content marketing involves creating and sharing valuable, relevant, and consistent content to attract and retain a clearly defined audience. This can be an effective way to attract and retain customers and drive profitable customer action.

Successful businesses often use a combination of these strategies in order to grow their online sales. It's important for businesses to regularly assess and adjust their online sales strategies in order to stay competitive and meet the changing needs of their customers.

Retargeting: Retargeting involves displaying ads to users who have previously visited a website or engaged with a business in some way. This can be an effective way to bring users back to a website and increase the likelihood of making a sale.

It serves the discussion to discuss how successful businesses engage digital transformation technologies in order to achieve sales growth?

Use technology to automate and streamline sales processes: Digital technologies can help automate and streamline sales processes, such as by enabling online sales or automating customer relationship management. This can help sales teams be more efficient and productive, and allow them to focus on high-value activities.

Leverage data and analytics: Digital technologies can generate large amounts of data that can be used to inform sales strategy and decision-making. Sales teams can use data and analytics to better understand customer needs and preferences, identify trends and opportunities, and optimize sales efforts.

Use digital marketing to reach and engage customers: Digital marketing technologies can help sales teams reach and engage potential customers in new ways, such as through social media, email marketing, or pay-per-click advertising.

Embrace new sales channels: Digital technologies can enable sales teams to explore new sales channels, such as online marketplaces or social media platforms. This can help reach new customers and diversify sales channels.

Provide training and support: It is important to provide sales teams with the training and support they need to effectively use digital technologies and adapt to changing customer needs. This might include providing access to learning resources or hiring a digital transformation coach.

Foster a culture of innovation: Digital transformation requires a culture that is open to change and innovation. Encourage sales teams to embrace new technologies and processes, and create a supportive environment that promotes continuous learning and experimentation.

**The case about Processes and systems for businesses in the online space:**

For business establishments, internally they had to reformulate their processes, policies, systems and automation thus prepare their business to address the new opportunities provided by digitalization and cutting edge technology disruptions. Similarly the processes in the sales function need to be completely robust and efficient using the right combination of automation and system software all of which optimize the order closure and product delivery and therefore optimize sales and the business potential in the larger sense.

To successfully acquire business from potential customers through B2B portals, businesses must streamline their internal processes, including standardizing quotations, promptly submitting offers with relevant details, clearly communicating pricing policies, and following up with buyers promptly. It is also important for businesses to track the potential conversions of leads obtained through these portals in order to optimize their results. This includes tracking the total number of leads obtained versus those that are potential leads (also known as "valid leads"), as well as tracking the conversion of valid leads into customer orders. By monitoring these parameters, businesses can increase the potential outcome of being part of a B2B platform.

To address risk mitigation, businesses should ensure proper documentation and online contracts, as well as effective customer complaint handling and reputation management processes. This can help to retain customers and maintain a good reputation.

How did the Online Business opportunity impact Business communication through websites, apps?

It is not in doubt that for online businesses increasingly website became the new marketing tool to directly acquire customers. Thus, online businesses had an imperative and dependance on website and the communication that is available about the business through the website. The information on the website had to align with the communication being made through the social media avenues. This was necessary to facilitate potential and faster sales closures and speedier customer acquisitions.

In sharp contrast conventionally SME business considered web site to be an investment with minimum function, or at best a tool for a prospective customer to generally understand the information about the company or verify the existence of the organization the case of many SME businesses websites were disconnected from the major business developments and in turn did not incorporate the developments with regard to the upgradation of the products and services, new customers signed up, testimonials for good quality given by customers, new accretions and certifications obtained in a timely manner.

Yet, it became evident that the Customers who prefer to buy online largely relied on the information published on the web site. If the information in the web site is well laid out, better and more informative, dynamically updated regularly so as to incorporate information which was current and latest, the chances of a prospective customer taking a purchase decision to buy from the company concerned is high. Website evolved with capacity to handle e commerce business where the customer was given the facility to directly order goods and obtain fulfilment thereon by directly transacting with the brand.

This became yet another sales avenue for many brands which also built a loyal customer base of customers acquired through their own e commerce sites. Many of these business failed to take due notice of the Online business opportunities that emerged as part of the digital transformation revolution. In actual reality, many of the aforementioned SMB businesses were substituted by their peer businesses and competitors in the same market place.

These businesses who embraced the opportunities unfolding through the digital revolution could surge ahead with exponential revenue growth and capturing customers and thereby the market share of erstwhile players who were completely out of business thus throwing them in deep financial crisis.

# Key Takeaways

**Entrepreneur qualities and their Origin**

Competent entrepreneurs possessing desirable entrepreneurial qualities such as passion for the business, risk taking ability, self-discipline, leadership, perseverance have a higher probability of success.

Origin and past background of entrepreneurs influence their attributes and temperament while they handle their role as an entrepreneur.

It is possible for entreprenurs to imbibe the ideal qualities of an entrepreneur and transform their personality to align with the new entrepreneurial role.

Through illustration, it has been demonstrated how entrepreneurs may have failed in their current entrepreneurial venture because of their not being able overcome their old attributes and temperament accumulated over earlier occupational stints as professionals or employees.

Entrepreneurs need to understand the qualities and attributes that can cause their failure and shed qualities that are inconsistent with their entrepreneurial vision.

**Elements of the Business**

A business is made up of different elements or facets such as Legal Business entity, managment and ownership structure, team members and Employees, products, solutions and services, customers, vendors, Lenders to the business, Physical assets and infrastructure, intellectual property owned by the business and so on.

Understanding and analysing the elements of the business is paramount in order to evaluate and understand the business.

Every element is important for the business due to their mutual interdependencies, inter relationships and synergies and all the elements together make the business organisation.

## Product, Customer and Market

Businesses need to align products and solution to meet the needs of the end customer and need to be clear about the latent problem that the solution is capable of solving.

Businesses need to assess and identify the strengths, limitations and lacuna, if any, in the existing products and solutions vis a vis competitors products and solutions and examine cost and price competitiveness in order to devise their sales strategy.

Through periodic market survey and analysis, businesses need to track their market share vis a vis competitors, market trends and business outlook and devise strategies that can drive growth.

Businesses may devise strategy to increase market share through the process of building a range of products forming a product mix which may comprise own manufactured products, strategic products, and outsourced products.

Businesses need to identify and understand which profile of customer actually derives the highest value from the product and solution, and which customer or market segment is not likely to derive value from the solution.

A business needs to identify its ideal customer, those who cannot be its customer, define loyal customer and devise key customer account management processes to leverage growth in sales.

Businesses need to identify if the business is in red ocean and need to devise strategy for competing in an overcrowded market place where the business faces multiple competitors.

Businesses need to recognise their product positioning in the market whether they are 'Me Too' products or 'Me Better' products.

Businesses need to identify their top two peer competitors in the market and make an in-depth study to understanding their business strategy approaches.

Businesses need to identify potential niches in the market that competitors have not tapped and evaluate business potential for their products and solution.

Technology backed businesses need to pursue opportunities for innovation and product development to create 'blue ocean market scenario' for their solution and experience huge business traction and customer acquisition.

Businesses need to understand whether the markets where they are currently operating are really scalable.

## Marketing and Sales strategies

Businesses need to create a Structured sales plan formulating strategic Sales Revenue goals aligned to business model.

Businesses must Formulate sales strategies contextual to a particular industry- adopt multiple sales avenues to engage with customers namely: Direct/ channel/ online/ exhibitions/ tender, in others, an Omni-Channel approach.

Business must create a revenue scalability strategy to ensure continuous acqusition of new customers as well as retention of existing customers.

Through a strategy based approach, businesses should facilitate Exponential growth in 'new customer numbers' on a period-to-period or quarter-to-quarter basis .

Businesses need to do the following:

To continuously track their value proposition vis a vis competition and ensure that the same stays intact through continuous new product development and innovation.

To align Sales function to engage customer retention strategy and customer acquisition strategy backed by relevant processes to expand sales revenues.

To define key sales Revenue objectives of the sales function covering sales revenues from Key customers, New Customers, Existing customers, New customers through AMC to be achieved sub goals target sales key customer a/c management, new market geographies as may be relevant to the industry vertical.

To establish sales processes covering customer Acquisition, Customer retention, install up-to-date systems, software and automation.

To establish sales and marketing protocols to manage and streamline reporting structures, inter departmental communication, better team work and balanced decision making.

To constitute sales team in conformity with a well thought organisation chart for sales department, with resources in team lead position, and back end coordinator resources handling coordination, and front end customer facing business development executives for complete effectiveness of team work.

To facilitate and enable continuous up-skilling of the sales team on sales domain and selling skills, and on the job training on the product and technology domain. '

To ensure a structured and balanced salary package and incentives for Sales personnel to ensure better sales team retention.

To foster a customer obsession culture, processes for greater customer retention; customer processes and mapping customer satisfaction and feedback.

To establish key performance indicators relevant to the sales discipline for effective key performance management.

To create sales plan needed to target increase in numbers of paying customers and to limit exposure to non paying and poor paymaster customers.

To ensure that Sales plan are aligned to the financial plan for ensuring equilibrium and total alignment to the business and financial goals.

To ensure that Sales plan are aligned with working capital objectives in terms of limiting exposure to credit Sales and Receivables and inventory control.

To ensure that their Sales plans are aligned to the operating model of the business and thereby ensuring quality and timely delivery of products to customers.

To leverage Pricing strategy and price policies to compete in the market with potential competition and protect market share.

To continuously track customer acquisition cost and work on acquiring customers who contribute higher to 'higher lifetime value'.

## Online Business

Preparing your business to address online opportunities is about a complete bottom up redefinition of the marketing sales and delivery department of the business and include after sales services also. from processes to policies, product literature to communication all the aspects have to be realigned to address online opportunities.

customer response system including speed of response to customer complaints and redressal, product rejections and product returns, product replacements need to be managed through robust systems. online businesses have huge opportunities for customer growth at an exponential rate there being no physical boundaries. in the online space different business models have evolved such as B2C B2B B2B2C and so on, and SME businesses need to leverage the above avenues to produce scalability. Online businesses need to make their communication robust, appropriately restructuring their branding and bring dynamism in their website and social media strategy.

Existing SME Businesses pursuing online business opportunities need to realign their businesses in terms of installing robust and efficient processes, and engaging systems and state of the art technology to automate tasks and digitalise records.

# Synopsis – Volumes Two And Three

**Volume Two**

Part 1 - Strategic Business Planning

Part 2 - Operations and Delivery Strategy

Part 3 - Innovation & Product Development strategy

Part 4 - Franchising strategies

Part 5 - Branding Strategies

Part 6 - Business Growth Strategies

**Volume Three**

Part 1 - Key Business Performance Indicators

Part 2 - Human Resources Strategies

Part 3 - Business Growth Strategies

Part 4 - Business Success and Business Failure

Part 5 - Top Rules for Business Success

# About The Author

Bala K N is a chartered Accountant and Legal professional with over 37 years of post qualification experience. After an inital stint in executive and managerial positions in leading Indian corporates, he has had an extensive career as corporate advisor and mentor to SMEs, Start-ups and NGOs.

Bala currently runs a consulting firm that advises and mentors NGOs, young entrepreneurs, with creating sustainable organisations, helping set them on their journey to exponential growth and achieve their goals. He has also founded a Law Firm offering Legal services to businesses.

He is associated with Angel investor networks and provides strategic thinking and expert inputs on the evaluation of potential start-up suitable for investment.

He is on the advisory board of an NGO operating in the field of mental wellness and empowerment of students and youth. He is a member of Rotary International and takes keen interest in associating with social impact projects.